Time to Remember

See photo page 6!

Time to Remember

SUSAN FORTUNE

Ian with love.

Susan Fortune

Published by Susan Fortune 2002
© Susan Fortune 2002

Photographs: 10 Akbar Road and The Church of theRedemption,
Bedi Films New Delhi

A CIP catalogue record of this book is available from the British Library

ISBN 1 899 47102 2

Designed by James W Murray
Set in Galliard
a contemporary adaption of Robert Granjon's typeface – drawn by Matthew Carter
Printed and bound in Great Britain by Bookcraft

Contents

For

David, Yaya and Johnnie

With Love

India prior to partition

Prologue

Commissioned into the Wrens in June 1942, I was posted to Immingham as a cadet officer until the confirmation came through. Immingham was a depressing place and I can only remember it as flat, dull and permanently foggy and the sea always a dreary grey. There were rows of Nissan huts, in which we worked and were housed. Our sleeping quarters in one of these huts consisted of bedrooms on either side of a long passage, at the end of which were the bathrooms. However everyone was jolly and fun to be with. We had some very amusing moments; one in particular still makes me laugh. I was in bed, when suddenly I heard screaming, I jumped out and rushed to find out what had happened and was met by this distressed Wren officer who gasped

'A man jumped through the window into my room'!

By this time all the other inmates had foregathered, and someone went to inform the Duty Officer but she seemed very uninterested. However the poor girl was very upset, and she spent the night with me. Next morning she was summoned to the 1st Officer who told her that she was making a bit of a fuss when all it was that a young sailor probably wanted to see a girl in bed. However this was not the end of the matter, her father happened to be an Admiral. When informed of the goings on he came post haste to Immingham and had the 1st Officer on the mat ... 'These young girls who had had sheltered lives ... And under your care etc. etc.' I wish we had been flies on the wall.

When my confirmation arrived I was the first to know, as I was on duty in the signal office when it came through. Admittedly the signal was addressed to the 1st Officer, but I thought it quite in order to telegraph my tailor in London to send my uniform forthwith – which is a lovely naval command. The post moved quickly in those days and I received it the next day so I put on the uniform before being officially told that my commission had been confirmed. In less time than it takes to tell I was summoned to the 1st Officer's office, who received me fairly coldly, and then – 'What did I think I was doing . . .' and on and on '. . . *and* before being officially told that my commission had been confirmed . . .' alas alack I thought, I shall be told to remove it – forthwith of course! However, her point having been made I was told I could go back on duty.

I was then, as a new 3rd officer, posted to H.M.S. *Wildfire* Sheerness in Kent. It was always referred to as Sheernasty – I can't think why since it was a very 'happy ship' – perhaps that was because we had a super Administrative Officer looking after us. It was also very near London and we could hop up there very quickly. We had the Hunt class destroyers based at Sheerness who patrolled the North Sea and their comings and goings were exciting and made us feel that we were part of things. Sheerness being a dockyard there were many ships in for repair or refitting. There were always 'H' boat submarines in dock – these were tiny submarines, which must have been very claustrophobic. They then, when fitted up or whatever, would disappear up to the West Coast of Scotland to do mysterious things. Our work was not very taxing though interesting as it was so immediate – it was mainly cyphering and de-cyphering signals to and from the destroyers on patrol, and being responsible for seeing that they got to the right person for action – otherwise it was routine signals to and from other dockyards and bases, for stores, equipment and matters of personnel.

We had a few excitements. We lay in the path of fleeing German bombers who, in order to get off more quickly when interrupted in their work by our fighters, would drop their undelivered loads over the Medway and us. We could hear the spent shrapnel of the anti aircraft guns pattering on the roof and the distant thrump of the bombs. If we happened to be on duty we would have to stay put until it was all over – Never did it occur to us that we might get hit.

Quite a few times escapees from Holland were rescued from their small boats in the North Sea and brought into Sheerness. One morning I saw three of these escapees being helped ashore, and one of them removed his woollen hat as he jumped on to the quay and a cascade of blonde hair fell out to reveal a girl. I often wondered what their story was. These people would then be taken up to London for debriefing.

There were a lot of very amusing and some very unusual personalities and we all got on very well. One was Stella Courage, quite a few years older than most of us, (she had 2 children, who had been sent to America for safety), and whose husband, a Naval Officer, worked in Combined Ops in London. Naturally, after night watch she jumped straight on the train back to her home in London for her 24 hours off. A notice had been promulgated that all Wrens coming off night duty must have four hours sleep or rest, which she always ignored.

Then one day this was discovered. A telegram was sent to her to return to duty 'forthwith' – the navy does love that word! Very quickly the reply came saying, roughly, 'please send luggage' I don't think any of us have laughed so much. She of course left the WRNS, but as we did not hold a King's commission she could not be court martialled. She then worked the rest of the war in the canteen in Combined Ops, where her husband was stationed. Before her departure her husband had gone out on one of the convoy destroyers on Operation *Torch* to North Africa and brought back a bunch of bananas for us – as no one had seen a banana since the war began, it was a huge treat. Stella would hold up the mantelpiece in the ward room to air her views and one of her best expressions was 'it's an absolute bug-aah' I thought this was wonderful and so sophisticated and grown up that I tried it at home – it was not a huge success – my mama got pink from the feet upwards. Another memory is the time when I was phoning to book rooms in London for myself and my then boy friend, who having just returned from an Atlantic convoy rang to say that he was coming up to London, and could I arrange accommodation. I booked myself in at Brown's and was about to make a call to book him in elsewhere, when the Wren officer with whom I was on watch, asked 'D'you mean you're booking rooms in different hotels?'

'Of course' I answered, blushing a bit, 'what do you do?'

'Oh,' she said 'I book a double room at the Mayfair.'

'D'you mean you spend all night with him?'

'Of course' she answered.

'What do you talk about?' said I, amazed.

'Talk?' she said her voice rising with incredulity 'we don't *talk*!'

How could I have been so naïve? My children were convulsed when I related that story.

The mess was in a row of period houses, two of which had been knocked together, there were not many of us and it was all very cosy, we could also have the odd person to stay over night There was at that time a lovely little song that Deanna Durbin sang – the first verse went:

> 'I'd like to climb an apple tree
> Though apples green are bad for me
> And I'll be sick as I can be,
> It's foolish but its fun,'.

This I would sing when and wherever, when I was full of the joys. One evening I came back off duty and found a note at the end of the banisters, which said

'Susan - go and climb your apple tree somewhere else, there's a baby in the house'!

We had two lovely rendezvous where we would meet our friends in London, Claridges and Fortnum and Mason. The Causerie at Claridges allowed you to eat as much as you wanted off the huge table of hors d'oevres for five shillings, while remembering not to order pudding or coffee as the bill soared up if you did that. Additions plus the cover charge was their method of overcoming the mandatory charge of five shillings (25p) for a meal, enforced during the war so that those more fortunate were not seen to benefit by getting ration-free food. Fortnums wasn't quite so formal, and we made friends with the waitresses there who were more than kind with little extras.

After a year at Sheerness I decided to volunteer for an overseas posting.

This story starts in August 1943, just before I joined Combined Operations in London as a Signal Officer and thence to New Delhi – my meeting Bruce and the magical life we led there together – the interesting people I met and exciting places I saw

I spent six months in Ceylon in 1944 where the HQ of SACSEA seemed to be staffed entirely with Admirals, Generals and Air Vice Marshals, and of course this was not so, it just seemed so. One day when I was delivering an 'Eyes Alone' to the Chief of Staff, General Pownall, his P.A. said rather sadly 'I do wish someone would call me sir'. I assured him that I would do so immediately!

Bengairn 19th July 2001

The Beginning

It was August 1943

I had been based at H.M.S. *Wildfire* Sheerness since I was commissioned in June 1942. Quite soon after volunteering to go overseas I was summoned to London to Combined Operations H.Q. to be interviewed by Captain Micky Hodges. RN and 1st Officer Heather Hayes WRNS for a posting to Mountbatten's new Headquarters in India. Micky was the Signal Officer in Chief COHQ Whitehall; we all at HMS *Wildfire*, knew about Combined Operations and Lord Louis Mountbatten and that he was going to be Supreme Commander in South East Asia. At the end of the interview Micky asked me if I would like to go to India by sea or air. My first reaction was, "My God, they're taking me on!" – I was stunned. I didn't even know where Delhi was –well not precisely – however I did not hesitate: I chose to go the more exciting way – by air.

As I was walking down Whitehall a little later, I thought but there will be no sea, no lovely destroyers steaming out with their slender bows cutting through sparkling beautiful bow waves, and I remembered when the Hunt Class left to go to North Africa on operation *'Torch' (Invasion of North Africa)*. It was a beautiful clear sunny morning. I was on early duty and as I arrived down at the dockyard I saw the flotilla leaving, steaming gracefully in line ahead out of the harbour and into the Medway. 'Whoop whoop whoo – oop' they screamed – it was very moving and as I watched found it hard to hold back my tears. It was many years after the war that Micky told me how I got the job with them in the first place.

Requiring an additional Wren Signal Officer to go to New Delhi, they requested HQ WRNS to send them a batch of reports, instead of having to interview a stream of Wren officers. My report, I was told, amused them and they decided to have a look at me. I remembered my annual report being read out to me *(normal procedure)* in July by our 1st Officer Hudson.[1] She touched on various points and then said 'I have given you a

---

[1] 1st Officer Monica Hudson – Our WRNS administration Officer at Sheerness (HMS Wildfire). I met her again many years later when she was staying with friends of ours in Scotland, by whom she was known as the Scharnhorst! She was large and ungainly but a lovely person and I was able to thank her - she was very amused.

high rating for leadership, but before you get swollen headed, I have added that this is mostly in the wrong direction.' I must to say I did not give this much thought, and little did I realise that it was to get me this fantastic posting.

On reflection I do not think that I 'mis' led anyone, though I do remember going on night duty in a jolly mood after a party on board one of the destroyers, and during the watch being given a signal to send to HMS *Cattistock*. This read: To HMS *Cattistock*: From C. In C. Nore 'On completion of patrol proceed to Harwich'– which we coded up. We all loved Lieut. MacFarlane its C.O., and I suggested we put a p.s. at the end of the signal, so added a couple or so of groups for 'Hi ya Mac'. If there were any repercussions we intended say that it must be corrupt groups for 'message ends', and with great mirth we sent it on its way and happily went off duty at 8 a.m. next morning.

How naïve we were. I discovered later that day that Captain (D), *(Captain of the Hunt Class Destroyer Flotilla)* the rest of the destroyers on patrol and East Coast land bases, including the Nore Command Chatham, at which H.M.S *Wildfire* was based, had all picked up and decoded the signal. Captain 'D' was furious. He broke W/T silence and sent a signal to the *Cattistock* 'Expunge all after Harwich'. Of course a copy of this landed in our signal office next morning. However nothing was said though much was rumoured!

A few nights later, again on night duty, I had to deliver some signals to the Commodore. When I opened the door of his office the room was in darkness, except for a green shaded lamp on his desk, and I quietly slipped the signals onto the desk, but he said nothing nor did he look up – so I crept silently to the door. Just as I got there he spoke, 'sending any more signals Mackie?' I froze. 'No sir', I said and fled.

Prior to my departure for India, I joined Captain Hodges' signals team in C.O.H.Q, which was in the then New Scotland Yard building in Richmond Terrace overlooking Whitehall. It was a warren of passages. There was a narrow door, in our very small office, behind which was a long narrow passage. From time to time strange people appeared and disappeared through it – they had nothing to do with our office – where they came from or where they went I know not. I was introduced to the high powered traffic that passed through – as a recent arrival, I was amazed at the 'hot' stuff I was allowed to read. I worked in a slight daze though I was very fascinated with everything going on and the laughter and banter that went with it.

Mountbatten left for India on 2nd October along with Captain Ronnie Brockman RN his secretary, Lt. Commander Arthur Leveson RNVR his Flag Lieutenant, Micky Hodges and his 2 i/c Heather Hayes and others. From our office – Gordon Blair, Margaret Maude and myself were to follow on 10th October, with a few other bodies from COHQ. Yvonne Stafford-Curtis, part of the signal office team, would remain behind and follow later by air (which incidentally took her several weeks of being shoved on and off seaplanes, as places on board became available).

Outward Bound for India

We left London on 11th October 1943. There were eight of us on board.
Group Captain Gordon Blair RAF Deputy Signal Officer in Chief COHQ
Margaret Maude Flt Officer RAF
    (later married Lt.Cmdr Arthur Leveson)
Susan Mackie *(self)* 3rd Officer WRNS
Commander Bousefield RN Paymaster
Lt Col Joe Weld, Intelligence
Another Wren Officer and two Naval Officers, whose names I forget.

We left Hendon in a Dakota, the eight of us on one side and the other was stacked with secrephones *(telephones which scrambled 'on line' between callers, and therefore conversations could not be picked up by unwanted interceptors)* etc for the Supremo.

Extracts from letters to my mother:
RAF Officer's Mess
Portreath, Cornwall

October 11th 1943
'I got someone to post a letter to you this afternoon just before we left. We are a day late as you may have guessed. Sunday was a rotten day. We had all foregathered at COHQ, but the fog was such that we were told to go home again for 24 hours. We didn't think that we'd get off today either, but the weather we were told was fine in Cornwall and if it cleared here we'd go. Eventually we left COHQ about 1030 though everyone was a bit pessimistic, the fog was still so thick here with us. We had lunch at Hendon and stooged around just waiting. We got off just after 4 o'clock and got right up above the clouds into brilliant sunshine. The clouds looked like

fluffy cotton wool beneath us and in the distance like snow covered mountains. As we flew over gaps in the clouds we could see the pattern of the fields below and the little villages which looked like toy towns.

The coastline was beautiful. The setting sun over the water seemed to be dipping right into it. The little coves with white flecked water, the quiet houses and villages were quite unreal and the streams were ribbons of light. This being my first flight I was surprised that there was no sensation of speed. One hardly knew one was moving. It took us two hours. I shall see nothing on the next lap and tomorrow morning we will breakfast in a very new place. After that we will be flying by day and have a bed at night. I will try to get a letter sent to you from our next stopping place, there should be someone going the other way. So don't get ideas into your head if you see an English stamp!

I managed to get out to Sheerness on Sunday p.m. as we had all been dispersed because of the fog. I wish you could have seen their faces when I walked in. Some of them had sent farewell telegrams! They thought I was my ghost! However I got a wonderful reception – I nearly wept. So did they! 1st Officer Hudson was sweet she just clasped me by the hand and didn't say a word. It was rather like coming home. Molly Gilbert is going to Londonderry, she'll enjoy that, it's the most popular place to go. I left just after 6 and got back to Megs *(my sister)* about 8.30. Being all alone in London made me feel so very depressed, I don't know why it should but it takes a nasty unshakeoffabble – is there such word – grip. In a few days time I will have seen lots and lots of exciting places and shall have heaps to tell you.'.

October 12th Between Gibraltar and Tunis
. . .'When we set off last night the moon was just breaking through the clouds and I could see the sparkle on the water below. Lights were put out as soon as we took off and we were allowed to take down the blackout. We rose right above the clouds into the moonlight, it was quite wonderful. The great expanse of cloud below us looked like ruffled snow. We all managed to make ourselves comfortable and sleep. *(We flew right out over the Atlantic before turning east towards Gibraltar, lest a German night fighter might be on the prowl)* The Canadian co-pilot gave me his fur-lined coat, I was most grateful. Though we wore parachute harness on the first lap, we now wore Mae Wests and looked like sides of houses! I woke about 5 a.m., we were still above the clouds and the moon, a bright orange, was disappearing into the thick of them. Later we were quite low over the

water and we could see some ships ploughing their way across with a great streak of white in their wake. The sky was streaked with hazy pink, grey and shades of pale blue, and soon the brilliant sun put a strong glare over everything. I felt very hot and had to remove my jacket.

It was a great thrill to see the coast of Africa ahead and on the other side, Spain. The earth is very brown and rich looking. Houses with red and ochre coloured roofs are dotted over the land. We circled round Gibraltar for some time as there was a mist clinging to the Rock. Eventually it lifted and we landed at about 10 a.m. Only then did I realise why no chances are taken landing or taking off. The runway is so short and one can tip into the sea very easily[1] The Rock was never completely visible at any time as the mist clung to the top. Unfortunately we had very little time before we took off again and we were whisked off by car accompanied by Group Captain Gordon Blair, who was acting as our nanny. We four girls were given a room with a bathroom and a balcony overlooking the sea. On our way through the streets we saw carts piled with bananas and grapes – you should have heard the shouts of joy coming from our car. However only having about half an hour to bathe and push down breakfast before being collected again, we hadn't time to stop. I asked for some cigarettes and the boy brought me up 50 State Express, price 2/1(11p). Does that not make you laugh? We were brought coffee, toast and lashings of butter and marmalade – so we ate with one hand and dressed with the other! We took it out to the balcony where we could look down on the huge harbour with all the lovely ships lying there. In the distance we could just see the coast of North Africa. The old Group Captain – not so old really – knocked timidly on our door, just as we were putting finishing touches to our faces, and asked if he could come in. Poor lamb, he'd been told that his breakfast had been sent up with ours. So we ushered him out to the balcony to feed on what we had left. It was really very funny. I must say he's being awfully sweet the way he's been looking after us. After breakfast we clambered back into the car and set off. We were so sad about the bananas and told Gordon that we must have some – so he told the driver to stop at the first fruit barrow and we hopped out, arriving back on the runway with a pile of bananas – wonderful.

Later
We are well up now, but there are very few clouds below, just small puffs

---

[1] General Sikorski, who was the leader of the Polish Government in exile, had done just that, fatally, a few months earlier.

here and there and far down I can see the ripples over the expanse of the Med. On our left stretches the long brown and white coast of Spain, but we shall soon leave that and be over Africa where we will fly along the coast until we arrive at Tunis. I cannot somehow feel that I am far away from home. I suppose that is because of the short time it has taken us to cover such a great distance. I was in London yesterday, which is a strange feeling.

I have just been up to the control room where I sat and listened to dance music on the radio. That was fun.

I am now back in my seat crouched up to the window with the sun pouring in. The land seems to move so slowly beneath us, there is no sensation of speed, though we are flying at 200 mph, only a slight rocking movement as if in a motor boat. The crew have changed into tropical kit and we have put on blouses and removed our stockings, though the sun's rays are warm it is still a tiny bit chilly – we are nearly at 10,000 ft – At the moment everyone is settling down reading or writing. For lunch – though I did ask the pilot for lobster mayonnaise and ice cream, and he said he'd do his best – we got cheese and hard tack biscuits – very dry and powdery when chewed, and hard to swallow. So much so, that when asked if I wanted more, my answer produced clouds of powdery crumbs right into Gordon Blair's face – much laughter.'

October 18th. Between Karachi and Delhi
'I have so much to tell of the last few days and I have seen so much. At the moment we are just taxiing off, it is just after 8 a.m. I wonder if you got my letter posted when we got to Tunis? It was strange to be there knowing that such a short time ago our troops made their triumphant entry. We drove straight to our hotel, and while we waited for our luggage a crowd of locals gathered round, staring at us as though we were out of the Ark.

Everything was remarkably cleared up, though many buildings, naturally, were down, and bits of wreckage here and there. We drove down the long tree-lined avenue that not so very long ago I saw the newsreel of the 51st marching down with the Pipes and Drums, a heart-warming and thrilling sight. We bathed and changed and were to foregather for a drink. I got down first and was told by the boys to hustle the other girls as they, the boys, were revelling in the sensation we were causing!

It was a wonderful moonlight night, with a deep velvety blue sky. The strange sounds and cries and the many lights fascinated me. I stood on our balcony and looked out on this strange place, and felt it was all a dream.

We left quite early next morning, and the whole of the next day we flew over the desert's empty battlefields. We passed all the famous places: Tripoli, Bizerta, Benghazi, Tobruk and Alamein. There was nothing much to see really except long tracks from tanks and trucks penetrating far out into the desert, and lines of fortresses outside the towns and places of battle. Here and there a burnt out tank or plane, otherwise it seems to have been cleared up.

We arrived at Cairo and as we jumped out on to the runway a blast of hot air greeted us. We were 25 miles out of Cairo, and having lost an hour on the journey it was dusk. The sun disappeared in about five minutes and we had stars over our heads and a most brilliant desert moon rising. We hung around a bit while waiting for things to be fixed up in hotels in Cairo. As we were a day late all our bookings had gone awry. We were all very tired and dirty and disreputable, but nevertheless happy and intrigued by everything around us. We clambered into our transport, which was a covered truck open at both ends. The heat was terrific, and a dry hot wind blew right through, bringing dust with it, making us even grimier. We drove along a straight road through the desert, flatness on either side and a great white moon shining in on us, and beating down all around. We passed the Pyramids – then the great thrill of driving into Cairo, lights blazing all round us – shops and open-air restaurants busy with people and noise, though it was well after 8 p.m.

We arrived at the famous Shepheards Hotel. Being a day late our bookings had been taken so we could not stay there, but at least we could eat. We were almost too tired by this time to care much about being tidy. We marched in as we were, covered in dirt and desert sand, to mix with the people of a city not at war and dressed in full evening clothes of pre-war fashion. We stripped in the ladies room to the amazement of some guests there. We washed, and tidied our hair, which had been blown to pieces in the open truck.

Then came the moment of money problems. We came back to the lounge to find the boys deep in calculation with some money they had managed to change. There was a wonderful garden restaurant with an open air dance floor and cocktail bar, most glamorously lit. We decided we could not afford the house charge for all this eastern glamour, so we had a jolly meal together in the inside dining room, after which bookings were arranged elsewhere to rest our weary heads. We were to be put up in the YWCA, (*Young Women's Christian Association*) the thought immediately filled me with horror, but it turned out to be absolutely wonderful with a super and motherly soul in charge – a lovely warm welcome for four very tired girls.

Next day we all met on the terrace at Shepheards. The heat was tremendous and we drank cool lemon drinks as fast as they could bring them. Gordon Blair had just bumped into his brother, he had no idea that he was there. The evening before, as we were sitting with pencils and paper trying to work out our finances, Margaret Maude was shouted at by a passing Naval Officer 'Good heavens Polly how nice to see you can you lend us some money?'[1] Her reaction made us rock with laughter. I didn't expect to see anyone I knew. However while sitting there staring into space and sipping my cool lemon drink, I looked up and there sitting nearby with two other Black Watch Officers was George Dunn[2], who is in the 5th Black Watch. I got up and walked over without saying a word to anyone. "Hello George", I said. He looked up. "My God, what on earth are you doing here?" he asked with as much surprise as mine on seeing him. So we all had strange experiences in this Middle East City. It really is a small world. We sat and talked and talked – about family, Arbroath and the Olivers. *(James Oliver was in the 7th Black Watch)*. He told me about their entry into Tripoli, how they slid in on a bright moonlit night. Having seen the place from the air, I could imagine it all. He'd been with Donald in Sicily just half an hour before he was wounded. They didn't think it was serious – but he died. *(Donald Murray who with the 5th Black Watch had gone out to the Middle East. with the 51st Highland Division in 1942, and had been a very dear friend of mine).*

The others.went into lunch, but kindly deposited my various goods I'd left at the family table, as I was obviously well settled in. *(Pat Douglas in the 1st Bn was one of the others sitting with George later to become Johnnie's godfather)* When I told them that I was going to Delhi, they said that Bruce Fortune, also in the 1st Black Watch, and who had been wounded, was going there to be an ADC to Field Marshal Wavell, who was taking over as Viceroy. He also said that George Cruikshank was

---

[1] Talking of money! – I started as a Wren rating with £2 per week, and as a 3rd Officer serving abroad this was increased to £25 per month.Derisory nowadays, at that time it was a huge amount.

[2] George Dunn was a young solicitor in Arbroath with the firm Oliver and Dewar. I met George when a young schoolgirl, when visiting Arbroath.with my father – who had been at university with James Oliver's father and Mr Dewar – I was stationed in Arbroath in HMS *Condor* before being sent to Greenwich Naval College in 1942 as an aspiring officer! While there the Oliver family was extraordinarily kind to me.

already there as an ADC, and gave me a note to give him. *(They had come from Sicily to Cairo to collect the battalion's bits and pieces which.had been left before Alamein and they were all now about to go home on leave. They would later set out on the invasion of Europe)* We all had a very boozy lunch, which was fun.

That night the family, as we had now firmly become, met at Shepheards at 7.30 to have a party to celebrate Gordon Blair's meeting his brother. As we were now in funds we fed and danced in the open-air restaurant. George Dunn, who was also dining there, came and asked me to dance. Gordon was impressed with his row of medals, which included the MC.

I had an awful fit of depression that evening, about what or why I know not. So did Gordon, but then he had just said goodbye to his wife and child. We started at the crack next morning and when we arrived at the aerodrome, discovered that there had been a hitch. *(Papers being taken 'by hand' for the Supremo, which were left at the airport for safekeeping, had somehow been put in an aeroplane flying westwards. There was much drama. We had to wait until they were recovered)* We sat about for about half an hour waiting to see what was going to happen. The long and short of it was that our journey was being delayed 24 or 48 hrs. So back to Cairo, singing songs all the way, the blazing sun pouring in.

We were wrecks when we got back to Cairo, but nothing daunted we flocked into the bank, in our slacks and hair all over the place, and changed money. Then we bathed and felt quite different. The next stop was a dhobie where left all our dirty clothes. I rang George to tell him we had been delayed and we arranged to meet at Shepheard's at 7.30. The family was all meeting at 7p.m. for orders, if any – there were none – so I left to join George and Pat.They were wearing their kilts and I was as proud as anything to be seen with them. We dined and danced at Shepheards, then went off to King Farouk's night-club, which was in the open air, and flood-lit, a deep blue starlit sky hung above us. All the lights, after the blackouts at home, are still strange to us.

Next morning we all met again at 12.30 and heard that we would be leaving next morning. After lunch Gordon and Joe Weld and two of us took a taxi to Mena House, a club just by the Pyramids. We bathed and then walked up to the Pyramids. I decided that I'd skim up one, but soon changed my mind! Gordon had been stationed there before the war, so he was a grand and an amusing guide.

All the Egyptian locals were very keen to show us inside temples, tell fortunes and various other things; we soon got rid of them. We had tea by the pool at Mena House, the air was pervaded by the heady scent of the frangipani blossom, a flower head dropped on to my lap, I put it in a ring of my gold chain which I was wearing. It survived several days!

Darkness was falling and the sky was banded with different shades of soft light, blue, pink and red. In the distance lights started twinkling, and the white painted houses stood out with muted luminosity. The dying light faded colours quickly from dusk to darkness. The Pyramids with their red gold stone were silhouetted against the fading light, and all round the sand became a dull gold. We walked down and round the Sphinx and by the time we got back to Mena House it was quite dark. A hot dry wind was blowing and made all of us feel rather tired and thirsty. Back to Cairo for dinner.

We took off next morning at 6 a.m. flying over desert land, which stretched as far as the eye could see. and shimmering heat seemed to rise from it. We landed at Habbinayah for lunch – leapt out of the plane into a searing heat. Happily, the. RAF Mess where we had lunch was air conditioned, and the relief of escaping the burning heat was a blessing. When we got back to the plane it was like going into an oven, we could scarcely breathe. Our lovely Dutch pilot, with the delightful name of Overander, said 'Quick, quick and I'll get you up to 10,000 ft in no time and you'll be cooler'.

And so on to Basra where we spent the night, or part of it. The Navy had been alerted and we were summoned to a drink party. It was a good feeling to be expected in the middle of nowhere and be feted. We were roused half way through the night to be emplaned and on our way to Karachi, where we arrived that evening. Our first taste – or should I say smell – of India. We were taken to an hotel where we dined and then retired to our room, which the four of us girls shared, but to all intents and purposes it was part of the public sitting room. Although there were walls on three sides, the door on the third was only amidships, so there was a space under and above what passed as a door. It was open to sights and sounds outside but I trust not to sights inside! At any rate it gave us a lot of amusement'.

October 20th
'... we flew to Delhi yesterday where we arrived at Willingdon airport. We were taken straight to Faridkot House where we were welcomed by Mountbatten's Flag Lieut. Arthur Leveson. *(the Supremo was on tour in Burma, and arrived back in Delhi on 22nd. His diary of that day says*

'coming back to Faridkot seemed like coming back home after all our adventures and I was glad to see that a new contingent of my staff had arrived from England'). We had tea and I found a letter from you which was wonderful. Later we went to our new home which is just nearby. It is or was an ex RAF Officers Mess and really very comfortable. We have a room with a bathroom (thunder box and a tin bath!) and a covered verandah.'

At first we worked at Faridkot House. Mountbatten lived there as well so it was all very chummy and a little chaotic. Mountbatten was, of course, madly good-looking, very friendly with a huge winning smile. He always remembered your christian name, which made you feel important. Everyone including LMB were constantly popping in and out of our 'office', which was really the Flag Lieutenant's room. I don't think any of us really knew what we were doing – I surely did not. After a couple of weeks we moved to North Block at the Secretariat, a huge and imposing building, with the even larger and more imposing Lutyen's Viceroy's House in the background. We had a fairly spacious office. Next door was Captain Micky Hodges RN, Signal Officer in Chief and our ringmaster.

First Days

When we moved to our office in North Block of the Secretariat – room number 147g – we got ourselves organised. Our duties as signal officers were to receive and despatch signals. We were responsible that the correct routeing – in other words by which means they went and through which channels – was on the signals before they went by D/R *(dispatch rider)* to the army cypher office in South Block, and woe betide us if we got it wrong. Incoming signals were decoded in the cypher office and delivered to us. On these we had to put the distribution list of offices concerned and 'for action' to the correct person. 'Eyes Alone' and 'Top Secret' had to be delivered by hand of officer. This we called doing our 'social rounds', and apart from a diversion it also gave us the opportunity to meet everybody, so that they were not just faceless people to whom we sent and received communications. We communicated with 14th Army Group who were in Burma, and other Army, Naval and Air Commands. Telegrams to the War Cabinet Offices were addressed to General 'Pug' Ismay, Churchill's Chief of Staff, and prefixed SEACOS – *(South East Asia (to) Chief of Staff)* and COSSEA – *(Chief of Staff (to) South East Asia)*, these were numbered and they went into the hundreds. Telegrams prefixed 'Eyes Alone' went only to the Supremo and there it would be decided what or what not the Americans could see, and accordingly deleted. The telegram would then come back to us to send to the appropriate American Office 'for information'. The same applied with the Americans. This always puzzled me as I thought we were fighting the same war!

We were soon joined by Sally Dean, our first American WAC – lovely Sally with her luxurious auburn hair and huge smile – a breath of fresh air. She was always laughing, noisy and so friendly, introducing us to the infectious greeting "Hi". I first met her when Admiral Jerram, who was a dear rather elderly and fatherly person to us all, had given me a lift back to the Mess. Sally was standing, with some other new arrivals, at the gates. The Admiral got out of the car and came round to help me out – I think his heavy gold braid must have impressed her and she may have wondered who I was, and not being acquainted with my lowly rank, I was greeted by the smartest salute. I never got another one! We shared a room for the first few weeks until the Americans had their own quarters. *(When Prince Philip of Greece arrived to stay with Lord Louis when we were in Kandy, he found her an amusing companion, and she received a letter, among a few, asking her out to dinner. "Gee" she said, when contemplating her reply "how do I address a Prince?" How we all laughed.)* She was soon followed by Yvonne Stafford Curtis (known as Yvne) after her long journey to Delhi being shunted on and off planes as places became available. Now we were five. The two senior signal officers (Heather and Margaret) worked days, plus one of us watchkeepers, but it was a few weeks before we started watches. The most taxing days of these watches was when we were on from 8am-1pm and back on duty the same evening at 7pm until 8am the next morning – and on night watch we were on our own, apart from our typists. We then had a day off and came back the following day from 1pm–7pm. Next morning the cycle started all over again. In order to have our Wren typists near at hand, a wooden hut was built on the flat roof outside our window and steps were made to go up through the open window and down onto the rooftop.

We were really quite busy, feeling our way as well, this being a new set up, with many of the Depts. starting from scratch. The Supremo was anxious to move everything to Ceylon so that we should be independent of GHQ, India. From our point of view it would be better as we would have our own cypher office, instead of having to rattle up D/R's to take papers to South Block or the chaprassis who shuffled to and fro and who, at night and in the cold weather, would be wrapped in a blanket and would delve into it's folds and produce a padlocked bag, for which we held the key. This procedure was carried out fairly silently as we could not speak Urdu and they could not speak English, so there was much gesturing and grunting (from them!) They caused much amusement. I often wondered what would happen of they decided to do a runner between the two Secretariats!

Letter to my mother
November
... 'Life is busy and exciting. We rushed round Delhi seeing all the wonderful sights. We're enthralled at the shops so full of things that we could not get at home. We bought material and had it made up into all sorts of clothes. We really all went a little mad. I had new white uniform skirts made because the regulation ones are rather thick and badly designed. Verandah dhersis *(tailors)* would sit on their hunkers on the verandah outside our rooms and stitch away on old Singer sewing machines. They would make a garment in a day – quite remarkable. They can also copy anything that they are shown. We all have bearers who look after our clothes, bring early morning tea and are generally at hand when needed. What was removed in the morning, was back washed and pressed by the afternoon. They move about very silently on their bare feet, their shoes always being left outside the door. Every morning after they have collected your early morning tea things, you'd hear them padding along the verandah, and then the noise of sloshing, as they put the dregs of everybody's cups into old tins, they then would stir vast amounts of the nasty damp and rather dirty looking sugar which we have, and drink it up – ugh. The other thing we have to get used to is their constant hawking and spitting – really revolting. If we want a bath we have to call for the pani wallah who comes trotting up and puts water into the tin bath, and later of course empties it. Strangely enough we don't find this unusual, and I have yet to find myself looking for taps! We are told that we shall be moving to Travancore House at the end of January. This is a lovely house which is the winter palace of the Maharajah of Tranvancore. Though called a palace it is in fact just a very large house set in beautiful gardens, with many large shady trees. The house itself will be our Mess and our quarters are being built in the gardens, a series of two storied buildings – and – we shall have proper bathrooms with running hot and cold water!
... When we arrived we were showered with invitations, it was incredible. Gradually after the first few weeks of accepting all round, we realised we

were going the way of all Delhi Belles and pulled in hard. We had our own particular circle of friends and stuck closely to them. George Cruikshank, who is one of the Viceroy's[1] ADC's, has asked me several times up to Viceroy's House to the cinema supper parties they hold. They were great fun – a car was sent to collect us and took us up to the House. As we drew up in North Court the chapprassis, sitting on their hunkers at the door, would spring into action, open the car door for us and the ADC alerted. We then had drinks and made our bobs to their Ex's, if they decided to be present, then had supper. There were usually about 20 or 30 guests and we sat at small tables of 6. Afterwards we went down to the cinema, which is down in the bowels somewhere. All very informal and relaxed – a change I should think from the previous Viceroy's parties.

... Brig. Guy Portman appeared in the office one day, I was surprised to see him – last time I saw him was in London last May, and had no idea that he was coming out here. He took me to meet the Spens' the family he is staying with. The father, Sir Patrick, is the Chief Justice of India; he is like Mr Pickwick, small fat and jolly. The whole family is so friendly and fun. Their son Michael is in the army and at GHQ. Joan his wife is very sporty and very easygoing. She is a great horsewoman and rides in point to points - very brave! They have two boys, Patrick and the youngest Michael only one month old. I have since seen a lot of them. Lady Spens told me that she hoped that I would come at any time and feel myself at home. I was quite overcome – and of course it was heart-warming to think I have such a lovely family to go to when I feel I need a bit of home life. They hoped that I would spend Christmas with them...

... When we first arrived the menus at the Imperial Hotel were enormous, several pages, which took us aback. This was soon stopped by the Viceroy who stipulated that there should only be a set menu, as there was a famine in parts of India – this was right, and made us all feel less guilty! What I couldn't understand was why or how in the hotels there were always intricate and beautiful designs down the centre of the dinner tables made of rice, which had been dyed many colours. Perhaps it could still be cooked and eaten when it was swept away!'

The Supremo left for Cairo on 20th Nov. to attend the meeting with Mr Roosevelt, the President of the United States, Mr Churchill, the Prime Minister, and Generalissimo Chiang Kai Shek, Commander of the Chinese troops. He came back on 28th, unhappy that most of his plans for

[1] Field Marshal Lord Wavell took over from Lord Linlithgow as Viceroy arriving in Delhi on the 19th October – by strange coincidence the same day as we arrived.

all operations appeared to be going awry. He spoke to us all to tell us that as so much landing craft, etc were to be diverted for operations in Italy and *Overlord*, (the invasion of Europe) he would have to think again. About this time I saw General Wingate[1] for the first time. He was walking down the passage in GHQ towards the Supremo's office, a strange rather twisted figure, and I swear he had a large alarm clock sticking out of his pocket!

December 28th   *Letter to my mother*

... 'On duty Christmas afternoon – Met Captain Squance, a U.S naval officer, who said 'Well, that's a marvellous Christmas present for their Lordships'. I didn't know what he was talking about – then he told me about the sinking of the *Scharnhorst*, and I nearly died from excitement. Isn't our Navy simply the most wonderful? The Brig collected me at 8 o'clock and we went off to the Spens'. I had a huge thrill before dinner when we heard the King's speech was to be broadcast – so often I have listened at home and thought of all our people listening overseas – and here I was! A cold shiver went all down my spine as I heard for the first time since leaving home the familiar Big Ben chimes and those wonderful words 'This is London'. It was a lovely dinner. The pudding arrived, blazing, the butler turned off the lights and it was carried round the table to much applause. It was all very festive and fun. Michael and Joan's month old babe is to be christened tomorrow – its various godmothers and godfathers were either in England or unavailable – so they asked me if I would be a proxy. Next day I was called for at GHQ and went back to the Spens' for lunch – as always I thought of home – cold turkey and more plum pudding for lunch. The babe looked so lovely in its long christening robes. Not a word or rather a sound from the child, he behaved quite beautifully. Just time to bath and change and off to do night watch ...

... Last week I asked George to have a quiet dinner at the Mess – it was my sleeping day as I had been on duty all night – I retired thankfully to bed with the lovely thought of a day's rest and quiet evening ahead. I was summoned to the telephone – it was George who told me to cancel dinner and put on my party dress – the new ADC had arrived and we were all going out for dinner and would call for me at 8.15. The Viceregal Packard came rolling up and out popped Felicity Wavell the Viceroy's daughter, and another girl followed by George and Hugh Euston, another of the Viceroy's ADC's, and lastly a tall kilted figure – very good looking, dark haired, with a moustache – I was introduced to the new ADC

[1] Wingate:- General Orde Wingate, leader of the Chindits

Bruce Fortune whom Pat Douglas had told me about in Cairo – that he had been badly wounded in North Africa and would be joining Wavell's Staff. His father, General Fortune, was captured at St Valery in 1940 when commanding the 51st Highland Division[1]. We all went to the Picccadilly. I sat next to Bruce, who is rather quiet but very attractive, and very easy to talk to. He goes off on tour shortly with the Viceroy. We had a very jolly evening and danced a lot – they were all so nice. Then off we slid home. When we came to the gates of the Wrennery our car was about to sail grandly through – but a guard stepped out and stopped us – he came up and poked his head through the window and said, rolling his r's to our liveried driver – 'You can't bring trucks in here after half past eleven!' – TRUCKS?! this was greeted with a lot of laughter, so George said at least he'd escort me to the door. We got out and started to walk through the gate only to be stopped again, this time with 'No gentlemen allowed in here after 12 o'clock'. We gave up and with 'hard luck old boy' coming from the car and much laughter from us all, we said goodnight'

Bruce was awarded an immediate MC on Jan 19th 1943; the citation read; 'Fortune was ordered to lead a daylight patrol forward to establish whether the enemy were holding a certain feature. The patrol had to move in full view of the enemy over open ground, and came under machine-gun fire soon after setting out. Yet Fortune managed to work his way forward to within 500 yards of the enemy position. From here he gained much valuable information, including the location of an anti-tank ditch, two machine guns and two anti-tank guns. He then skilfully extracted his patrol from the position, though on the way back it again came under heavy machine-gun fire. At this point some British tanks moving forward to recce the same positions came in sight. Ordering his patrol to keep under cover, Fortune ran under heavy fire to warn the tank commander about the anti-tank ditch and guns; in doing so he was severely wounded but, in great pain, continued until he had reached the leading tank and delivered his warning.'

Bruce told me of that day and how lucky he was in many ways; that he was picked up so quickly, that there was a hospital at the forward base, a brilliant Australian surgeon in attendance (whom he would have dearly liked to meet to say 'thank you') and the presence of the newly formed

[1] Rommel's letter to his wife after the surrender at St Valery, dated 11th June 'during the next few hours no less than 12 generals were brought in as prisoners . . . A particular joy for me was the inclusion of General Fortune Commander of the 51st British Division.' *Rommel Papers*

Field Blood Transfusion Units. He had been shot through arm, base of left lung and the liver. The last thing he remembered as he was hoisted onto the bonnet of a jeep, he told me with a laugh, was his platoon sergeant's voice, saying "jings he's fair riddled" as he slapped a note on his forehead with GSW (gunshot wound) for the medics. He always made light of this. Once when asked what part he played in the action at Homs, he replied "By doing something very stupid". Many weeks later he was sent by hospital ship to South Africa to recuperate where he remained for many months. The 51st Division having fought in Sicily were, in October, on their way back to the U.K. to prepare for the invasion of Europe In June 1943 Field Marshal Wavell was appointed as Viceroy of India and was to take over from Lord Linlithgow, in October. Bruce was asked to be one of his ADC's and he arrived in Delhi in December.

1944 started very quietly. New Year's Day found me on duty in the morning followed by night duty during which I felt awful, and spent the next two days in bed feeling pretty miserable. However, I was back to normal by 4th and back on duty

January 11th 1944
Yvne and I went over to Faridkot House at 1130 to have a bath – Arthur Leveson met us and led us to his room – it seemed odd that we used that as an office when we first arrived last October. Coffee was laid out for us. It was heaven to be in a long bath again. Back on duty, not very busy. We have a Commander Nott in the HQ's somewhere, I'm not sure what he does, but he rang our office – I took the receiver up "Supreme Commander's signal Office" I answered. "Not here," said the voice. "Oh," I said and put the receiver down. How we laughed. He did ring back again and we did let him speak! A note arrived in the office from Bruce asking me to come up to VH for dinner with him and Hugh – he is leaving in a few days on tour with H.E. He says I am difficult to get hold of, but sadly as neither of us work regular hours it's a case of him on duty, or me. He sent a car for me at 7 o'clock and we went first to a drink party given by Pamela Humphreys *(Wavell's eldest daughter)* and after dinner went off to the Picadilly – it was a really lovely evening. Bruce is so attractive and has such a wonderful smile. He goes on tour with HE next week.

January 22nd
What a day of heartiness and how I longed to back out of the 'all in' game

of mixed hockey – I must have been mad to say I'd take part – I hate the game! I lay down after lunch hoping wildly I might oversleep and miss the boat. Was delighted when it started to rain – but the game still held. Shivering and miserable, I climbed into the open transport and we rattled up to GHQ – 5 women and 15 men – it's suicide. However, I was not over-energetic and ran well away from the ball when it came my way! It started to teem with rain as we came away and the smell of earth and trees and freshness was wonderful and it made the effort worthwhile. I managed to have a bath and that was no mean achievement. Went up to C in C India this evening – a beautiful house and much more informal than Viceroy's. Lovely dark panelling and a heavenly old dining room – high ceiling – large fireplace and huge blazing fire. Dinner was fun and quite hilarious. Auchinleck is such a dear he is so cosy, charming and friendly to all us young things, not bit as one might imagine the Commander-in-Chief of the army in India to be. Admiral Maude and AVM Pierse[1] were there. After dinner Alex[2] and I went to the cinema to see a film which was worse than awful. News was of the invasion of Sicily informing us that events were moving so fast that more than likely this would be old news before we saw it – only seven months!!

January 25th
... Duty afternoon. Everyone in great form. Heather[3] very excited – lucky devil she is going home – Margaret and Arthur have decided to get married on 18th March – Yvne meeting heart throb, and I heard that Hal Grant[4] is taking *Mercury*[5] to Ceylon to see how the Signal Department is getting on in the new HQ, and others looking at other developments. – Suggested that I went too –'Why not' said Heather. How fantastic, I only said it in fun, but I could do with a few days leave. Made two long distance phone calls, one to Hal in Calcutta – very clear – people do move around – and one to MH in Bombay. I think that I am very lucky – I wonder what I shall think of all this in a year's time.

[1]Pierse - Air Vice Marshall, Allied Air C in C (he ran off with General Auckinleck's wife Jessie)
[2]Alex – Alex Greenwood ADC to Auchinleck.
[3]Heather was going to the U.K. and on to Washington with General Wedemeyer and party to present LMB's views on South East Asia strategy to the P.M. and the Combined Chiefs of Staff in the USA (codename AXIOM).
[4]Hal Grant – Colonel US Army Deputy Signal Officer in Chief and pilot of the Mercury – affectionately known as Little Hal.
[5]*Mercury* – a Dakota plane filled with signal equipment in order that the Supremo could communicate with us when on tour.

January28th
Night watch – 0035 – we're off! I *am* going to Ceylon – all is arranged, and we go on 30th. Invaded in the wee small hours by Hal, Jasper and party – to make arrangements for our ETD etc.. I'm so terribly excited and happy- at the thought of seeing the sea again – just imagine flying 1500 miles for two days – it's wonderful. Couldn't do much work after that.

January 29th
Up fairly early and started packing for the great move to Travancore, must do as much as possible before I go to Ceylon as I shall have only one day when I get back. It's amazing how much I've collected – and how bare my room seems now. Afternoon duty – not very busy. Party came back from Australia. Out to dinner with George and Co. Back early. Everything ready for tomorrow's early start.

– Off to Ceylon!

Visit to Ceylon

January 30th 1944 (letter to my mother)

'... I was wakened at 6.15 – it was cold and pitch dark. I got into slacks and had breakfast. My bearer Amir thought I was going on a terrific trek, and crept about after me in an awed way! – Very amusing. He took my case to the car where Sales *(Mountbatten's driver)* was waiting, and stood by until I was ready to go. It was still dark as we drove off – but faint tinges of light were appearing on the skyline and ground mist lay heavily all round.

We arrived at the airport and *Mercury* was there waiting. The runway was floodlit and all round were sparkling lights. A little way off Safdar Jung's tomb stands above everything – the towers and the dome illuminated by red lights *(these lights were to indicate position to approaching aircraft)*– it looked very eerie against the dark sky. The rest of the party started to arrive, Wren Macleod, who was going to Colombo for her Selection Board, Colonel Grant USA, Deputy Signal Officer in Chief and known as Little Hal, his co-pilot, gum chewing Jasper Vaughan USA, whose jaws were in perpetual motion – fascinating, and a boring naval surgeon called Birt – who I suppose came to see that we were mosquito free or something when the HQ moved to Ceylon!

It started to get light very quickly, the sky was streaked with smoky pinks and blue, and the darkness was being swept away. At last we all climbed in – the doors closed, the engines started and without noticing we found ourselves airborne. The sun had still not risen and the ground was still dusky and full of strange shadows. Suddenly the sun popped up over the horizon – a tiny edge of fire – and dusky red clouds swept across it. It moved quickly up free of the earth – an extraordinary sight – it only took seconds and during that time everything below us became transformed with a veiled red. Every pool every building was tinged with pink. As the sun rose higher it become a brilliant golden globe, gradually fading to an almost colourless but blinding light. The little villages scattered about seemed circled with mist – which was in fact just the lingering smoke from their fires in the still air. Trees seemed like little puffs of green and brown, their shadows thrown on the ground by the early morning sun.

MERCURY – Mountbatten's signal plane.
Heather Hayes and self October 1943

Faridkot House.
Mountbatten's residence
in New Delhi.
The cinema parties were
held in the open air on
the flat roof on the right

Secretariat GHQ
North block.
Staircase to our office

Yvonne Stafford-Curtis
Ronnie Brockman

Margaret Maude Sally Dean Heather Hayes
in no. 147g North Block

Visit to Ceylon Jan 1944. At 25 Mile
Surgeon Capt. Birt RN, Hal Grant, self

West front of the Viceroy's House from the Mughal Gardens, ADC room on the left at the end of the pool

Viceroy's House

Staircase to staterooms

State dining room

Durbar Hall –
used for
ceremonial occasions

The Viceroy with Bruce – South Court Viceroy's House. Taken by Cecil Beaton

19 Akbar Rd. Residence of Sir Patrick Spens, the Chief Justice of India

March 1944. Pipes and Drums of the 2nd Bn. The Black Watch
on leave from Burma, play in the Mughal Gardens Viceroy's House

The Pipes and Drums of the Black Watch with the Wavells April 1944
Archie John Wavell 1st back row, Bruce *far right back row*

Mountbatten in his office

King's Pavilion –
Lord Louis' residence
in Kandy

Dining room
King's Pavilion

7

Johnny Papps and Hank Hanbury
with the 'doodlebug' at K.P.

Lt General Wedemeyer U.S.A.
in his office Peradinya Gardens
Kandy

KANDY
CEYLON   Micky Hodges

8

RANIKHET July 1944

Sir Patrick and Lady Spens

Taken on our last morning on leave and known as 'the woodland idyll'

Hyderabad December Dec 1944
'…two princesses of noble bearing and wondrous fair…'

Princess Niloufa   The Princess of Berar with the Viceroy

Bruce, Hugh Euston, The Viceroy and the The Nizam of Hyderabad

10

Imphal 14th December 1944 – Lt.. General Slim C in C 14 th Army is knighted in the field by the Viceroy.
On the same day the Viceroy also knighted Lt Generals Christison, Stopford and Scoones.
Pictured above Lt.General Slim, the Viceroy, Bruce, *behind the Viceroy,* and Mountbatten. *on the right*

Jaipur House. *(back row 2nd from left)* Christine Guthrie, Self *(second row far right)*

Tiger shoot Nepal January 1945
The Viceroy sets out

All aloft in the howdah – Bruce, Felicity Wavell, the Viceroy Lord Wavell and the Maharajah of Nepal (*Joodha*)

Nana, who drove us

Viceregal
Knitmatgar

Rhamet
our faithful bearer

Selves with Jeannie our dachshund at the swimming pool V.H.

13

Viceregal Lodge Simla

George, self, Douglas Currie, Bruce and Freya Stark, just before Ghandi arrived, July 1945

Bruce   Pundit Nerhu   Charles Rankin

Pundit Nerhu leaving Viceregal Lodge

**SIMLA
CONFERENCE**
June / July 1945

Pundit Nerhu on his way, in a rickshaw drawn by four viceregal coolies

The Viceroy with
Mahatma Ghandi

Simla Conference
June/July 1945

Douglas Currie and
The Viceroy with
Malik Hyat Tiwana

The Viceroy with Mr Jinnah

Bruce's last public duty as ADC 23rd Sept 1945.
Presentation by Lt Gen Wheeler of the Legion of Honour to Wavell and Auchinleck.
Front row Auchinleck, Wavell, Gen. Wheeler.
2nd row, 1st Buchan *3rd* Douglas Currie *4th* Bruce

Buchan and Bruce leading the Viceroy and Gen. Wheeler round the Guard of Honour

Church of the Redemption New Delhi

His Grace The Bishop of Lahore

Bruce and Hugh arriving at the church

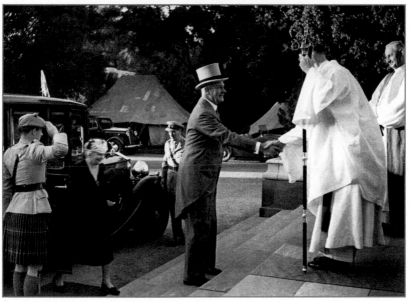

Colin Mckenzie, Lady Wavell, Douglas Currie, The Viceroy arrive and are greeted
by the Reverend J.D.Tyler who assisted the Bishop at the marriage service.

Being welcomed by the Bishop

The reception with our bridesmaids Cristine Guthrie *left* and Suzanne Marshall *right*

Going away
'... the final viceregal touch ...'

South Court where we left V.H. to go away. Cecil Beaton's photograph of Bruce
with the Viceroy was taken at the top of these steps, on the left

Point bungalow Government House Bombay.
The background, when lit up at night was known as the 'Queen's necklace'

The Vista *(Kingsway)* taken from the cupola of Viceroy's House
looking down towards India Arch. Jaipur House was on the right of India Arch and
our office was in the trees on the left just beyond the gates to Viceroy's House.
The Jaipur Column is in the foreground

Corner of the round garden, Viceroy's House. These beautiful borders surround the pool

A little further south it became cloudy overhead which all lent to the beauty as it formed a dark roof over our heads, and on either side miles away was clear sky sending down shafts of light on to the patterned world below. After a while I went forward and ousted Jasper from his seat and sat beside Hal – there I had the whole world in front of me and immediately outside the window the squat nose of the plane and the whirring propellers at either side. Ahead was a range of mountains; a deep river valley ran between them, which was covered in misty white dew that looked like billowing clouds. The sun poured through the gaps in the dark clouds on to valley below. The sun was not yet high enough to put everything into flat unshadowed form – but every bump stood out and there were patterned shadows everywhere, it was breathtaking. At one point was a memorable sight. Above and all round us were dark clouds – ahead, falling for thousands of feet, was a curtain of rain. Suddenly a gap in this veil of rain showed us a world beyond bathed in sunshine; it was like looking into another world of light and happiness. For some time after the way was uninteresting – great stretches of flat earth in monotonous shades of brown. A cloudless sky that mingled into a haze with the earth – everything was brown and dusty. Great riverbeds veined the land – most of them dried up. Here and there was vegetation round a village. One moated town we looked at through binoculars – it was Hyderabad – was walled round and had three of the most colossal palaces. In the wall above the moat was a huge white gate. It seemed so far away from everywhere and still that barbaric loveliness in the midst of it all.

Again hundreds of miles of barren country. I dozed off with the hot sun beating through the window. About 4.30 a great band of blue came into sight – the sea. It was wonderful to see it again. We were approaching over Madras and the Falk islands and we were soon over the sea – it sparkled and rippled thousands of feet below. To our left was a chain of islands – hardly islands, but patches of golden sand that stretched from the mainland to Ceylon. Everything was so clear and we could see for miles. A huge range of dark rugged mountains suddenly seemed to spring out of the sea on the horizon. I could hardly believe that we were really approaching the magic island of Ceylon – it seemed so impossible – but there it was in all its tropical beauty. We flew all along the coast – it is truly magnificent.

I have never seen such lush vegetation, every imaginable shade of green. The coastline is all coves of oyster beds and rice fields, the latter mostly underwater. Those that were drained were the most indescribable shade of soft spring green. Coconut groves were prolific – long straight lines of feathery palms, and here and there red roofs gave added colour. Jungle further inland stretched for miles and beyond that the high mountains. There it was below, before, and around me – everything so rich and fertile. The deep blues of the sea – the pastel soft greens of the rice fields – the varying greens of the palms and tropical growth. White houses with their red roofs dotted about in the background and the impenetrable smoky blues of the mountains, some with cottonwoolly clouds clinging round their summits. All this bathed by the brilliant sun. – magic.

Poor Macleod was very sick the last two hours as it was very rough going as is usual in very hot climates. We bumped about like anything. I did not notice when the plane lifted up in an air pocket but when it dropped suddenly like a double quick lift and then rocked from side to side, you've had it if you are at all inclined to be air sick! The poor girl was stuck in the little girl's room at the back. I went along to see what I could do. The tail of the plane is worse than anywhere in rough weather – one swings about and it is difficult to stand up. In normal weather Hal always knows if anyone goes to the loo as the tail of the plane wobbles. Eventually I got the poor child out and laid her down on some greatcoats, which we made into an improvised bed. Talking of the 'little girl's room', this is Little Hal's expression. Up in the cockpit every movement is registered on one of the whatnots, and if the instrument is not righted again, the plane would eventually go off course. Every now and then Hal, in his heavenly drawl would say 'someone has just gone to the little girl's room' or 'what are they doing back there? – playing hockey?'

Once or twice I went aft and we spoke to each other through the intercom. Other times I sat up front with the earphones on and tuned into dance music, which came through from somewhere extraordinarily clearly. I felt Hal nudge me, I looked over and he mouthed 'may I have this dance?' We sang with the band and then to my amazement I heard 'This is London calling to all Forces in the South West Pacific' After the programme finished I heard Big Ben strike. I can't tell you how thrilling it was – to be flying over India and to hear London – but I would think of something dramatic like that, wouldn't I?

We arrived at Ratmalana at about 6.30 and hopped out into the sweltering heat. I felt rather silly having my jacket and greatcoat handed down to me when everyone on the ground was in light tropical kit. It made me feel as if I had just come from the North Pole!

It was a lovely drive into Colombo. Huge trees and foliage hung over the road. Palm, cypress and bamboo. At the side of the road were lots of tiny houses, and shops selling fruit of every kind.. The whole atmosphere was so much cleaner than that of India – except for the fact that we still saw women sitting on their hunkers beside the unconcerned children – picking fleas out of their hair! – it made me shiver.

Arriving at the Mess out of the blue, the Wren officers were most awfully nice and I was treated like an old friend, given a room and every attention. Incidentally practically the moment I stepped into the Mess I met a girl I knew at home, and by the time I left discovered three more! I changed into my evening dress – the heat was terrific and so humid – there was a fan in the ceiling, but it only helped when I was in the firing line. I was called for later and we went to the Galleface Hotel, where the rest of the party was. The hotel is right on the waterfront. The moon was nearly full and the sky a deep deep velvety blue. I heard the sea and breakers, the roar and swish of the water as it rushed up the shore and sighed back again, it was like music. The moon laid the most wonderful trail of shimmering white, right from the horizon to the water's edge. The palms were silhouetted against the light as they leaned over the water, which was sparkling and white flecked in the brilliant moonlight. It was so still – just the sounds of the water broke the silence as the breakers came and went. I was struck dumb with the magic of it all. Now and then a small sail ship would cross the white trail of the moon on the water.

After dinner we all went out, I took my shoes off and felt the warm sand on my feet. I could only stand and gaze. There was a gentle breeze blowing and it touched my face. It is true what they say of tropical moonlight – there is something unearthly that goes with it and comes over you.

Next morning, everyone but myself and Jasper Vaughan, was busy. He collected me and we went to the Galleface, where we changed in to swimsuits and walked out onto the sands. We were told that the bathing was dangerous, but those huge bubbling breakers looked so tempting. I wandered in and out of the water to get wet. The water was warm and very blue. I lay on the sand, blissfully happy. Quite close to us lots of little Singhalese boys tumbled about in the sand and dashed in and out of the water. How free and happy they are running about naked, fighting, playing and carefree. I made a sandcastle much to their amusement. There is a large Palm tree close by that bends right out over the sea, how lovely it looked against the blue of the water. Some sailships moved slowly by and I saw one huge H.M. warship go into the harbour *(this turned out to be the H.M.S. Renown)*. Lovely to see ships again.

After lunch we all piled into cars and set off for the hills. We motored along by the shore for some time before we struck inland. The climb was gradual or seemed so – but suddenly we were high up looking down into the most heavenly valley. At 25 mile, as it is called, we stopped. There we found a huddle of giggling boys and girls selling fresh pineapples, cashew nuts and coconuts. We sampled them all, and took lots of photographs, whilst they giggled. I spotted one small boy standing with his finger in his mouth looking absolutely awe-struck, went up to him and bent down towards him, and with a terrified expression he burst into tears and ran to his mother and buried his face in her skirts.

It got much cooler as we climbed. The trees were lush and colourful, Flame of the Forest was covered in red blossom, and others had long tendrils of flowers hanging right to the ground. I welcomed the cool breeze because already my folly of lying in the mid-day sun was telling, and my back and arms were on fire and rather painful to touch. We stopped further up and looked back down the valley. In the distance was Sugar Loaf Mountain – round us green and rugged mountains and above us a white winding road. We passed tea plantations and some tobacco farms. The tea terraces were like rows of pale green necklaces.

We arrived at Kandy about 6 p.m. and were met by Michael Jacobs, who is overseeing the planning of our new H.Q. I feel very privileged to be part of the reconnaissance party, even though it was a bit of a con to give me a few days leave! The Queen's Hotel where we are staying overlooks Kandy Lake. The hills surrounding rise almost from its shores. The sun is setting – I cannot see it but its rays are tinting everything. It is cool here. I had a bath then went to M.J's room, where we all met for a drink. From there we could see the lake sparkling, with the light of the moon reflected in it. Later we had a hilarious dinner – being the only female I had to play mama. It had been a long day and I was very tired, but promised Hal to be with him at 9 oclock the next morning to go to Peradeniya and go round the sites with him as his unofficial secretary.

Next morning up very early, and skipped breakfast. It was a glorious day – it was also one of interest and a certain amount of mishaps. I rang for the boy and gave him my uniform to press. What did he do?– he put it in the wash tub! Happily everything dries very quickly in this heat, but I was hopping mad. As a result I missed my promised 9 o'clock R.V. and got down at 11. I was driven to Peradeniya Gardens where I met Hal. He shook his head sadly at my efficiency!

How wonderful those gardens are – and to think that we are going to work there. The buildings are coming on, the only ones built of brick were the Supremo's, the Communications Block and our offices, the rest were basha huts – made of bamboo or similar, pleated reeding – scattered about the gardens. Paths leading to the various offices were all named after streets in the USA and GB. There were little men scurrying everywhere. I think we have taken the place by storm – or certainly will do when we start arriving. We were surrounded by every exotic tropical tree and plant you could think of, and in every imaginable colour. Not far from where our office will be is a steep drop down to the river which runs by the gardens. The Wren quarters are to be quite near the gardens, though we shall be quartered at the Queen's Hotel in Kandy. So it will be a fairly scattered community, though no doubt a happy one. One of the chaps we met on site there was from M.G.M Studios sound Dept. He was most interesting and we had a long chat about various Stars. Most of the party knew what they were doing – I did not.

I tried to look intelligent and not make it too obvious the fact that I was there was a 'swan'[1] on my part! After lunch we were off again – what it is to be whipped about in staff cars! We sang songs nearly all the way down – stopped again at 25 mile and had our pineapple – which is left with its stalk, and the outside sliced off, so it is eaten rather like a lollipop – the girls giggled more than ever.

We went straight to the Galleface and had a cool orange on the terrace looking out over that heavenly sea. Then I dashed back to the mess to collect my evening dress. Bathing facilities were not so good there and one of the officers, who was overseeing the building of the new SEAC HQ, who was our host, and billeted in the Galleface, kindly offered me his room and bathroom to change in. He said he'd have his bath and clear out. I arrived well after the agreed hour and was told by the boy that he had left, and a bath was being run for me. I trotted gaily in, gave my dress to the boy to get pressed, got into my dressing gown and started laying out all my aids to beauty, then into the bathroom to get things organised. While I was in there, I heard someone come into the bedroom. Thinking it was the boy with my dress I took no notice. A couple of seconds later I bounced back into the bedroom and at the same time this other body bounced round the door into the bathroom. It was perfectly timed – and there we were, two dishabillé figures, face to face. One the owner of the room and the other the intruder – ME. We gaped at each other and then, after the initial shock, collapsed into the nearest chair in uncontrollable laughter. If you

[1] A 'swan' (swanning around) giving the appearance of working while doing nothing very much.

could have seen his face – I wonder what mine looked like. The funniest thing would have been if I'd been in the wrong room! But that would have been too much like a play. I discovered to my comfort that I had not pinched his bath, but he'd been called away to the telephone before he'd had time to dress. For ages afterwards every time I thought about it I laughed. He gave a wonderful party for us. We had drinks with him and then went to the Silver Fawn known as the Septic Prawn, where we dined and danced. What fun it was. I tried to think of everything from a distance – I visualised Ceylon on the map and tried to believe that I was really there, it really did feel strange.

I was called for at 7 o'clock the next morning, back into *Mercury* and we took off. It was indeed a whirlwind trip. I found it hard to believe I'd really been there – and strangely it seemed ages ago since I'd set out. I felt awfully tired, so lay down at the back of the aeroplane amid all the signal equipment and fell asleep. When I woke I felt a different woman. Back to my station in the cockpit beside Hal. He let me 'drive' for a bit. I was scared stiff. He went to sleep, or pretended to, having given me instructions such as: 'if the needle starts going to the right turn it back'. However 'George' was switched on so I was quite safe! I think I told you that on the way out from England to Gibraltar we were on automatic pilot. Fortunately I was unaware or I'd have had fifty fits thinking that we were flying without a pilot on my maiden voyage. But I'm getting blasé now!'

Delhi Days

Diary

February 2nd

We arrived at Willingdon on the dot of our E.T.A. Col. Boileau met us with Hal's car. Arrived looking an awful mess at the Wrennery, spied Admiral Somerville just in time and shot out of sight! Changed and went straight on night duty. A note was waiting for me from Bruce asking me to come up to see round the Viceregal Gardens. Having only been at VH in the evening, I look forward to seeing them. I am on duty tomorrow afternoon but arranged to go out with him tomorrow evening. I told him I'd just come back from a two day visit to Ceylon – and of course he has just been hundreds of miles on a 12 day tour with H.E. to the U.P and Bombay – ah well I'll just have to be content with being impressed with myself. Heather is in a state of excitement about going home on '*Axiom*'. Most Immediate came through for the Supremo and I phoned Micky Hodges, as I thought the '*Axiom*' party were leaving tomorrow and I'd better have it delivered – but he said the date has been put off until 5th – no one told *me*! Hurriedly wrote a letter home for them to take – there was no other excitement during the night.

February 3rd

Bed most of the day. Chris Morton – *(my stable companion after Sally Dean joined her compatriots)* – and I burnt the last of our wood and had a blazing fire, and drank the last of our gin as a final gesture Bruce called for me at 8.15 and we went straight up to V.H. – had dinner in his room, the table laid for two, was drawn right up to the fire – it was heaven and we had a lovely dinner. He is rather shy, but so nice. Then went and danced at the Piccadilly and afterwards drove out to Safdar Jung. We climbed up the tower and saw the whole place under moonlight – it was very beautiful but very eerie as there are so many ruins around it. It was a lovely evening.

February 4th Move to new Mess at Travancore House

Place in pandemonium this a.m – trucks, vans and tongas helping the move. The household was lying in the driveway waiting shipment. How bare everything seems. Got into slacks and had breakfast and finished packing odds and ends. Amir fetched a tonga *(two wheeled horse drawn buggy)* and took our cases to our room in our new home. It came back for Chris and me and we went clutching our final oddments. The road was a stream of tongas ferrying Wrens and their belongings. The place is very damp and very strange. We unpacked and had lunch – amazingly that was laid on. Duty all afternoon, got home to find the rooms full of smoke – no hot water – absolute chaos, and I was due to be with the Spens' at 8pm. I phoned Sir Patrick and told him my plight – he sent a car for me and I bathed and changed there. We all went to the Gymkhana for dinner – I ate 9 oysters!

February 6th

On early. Changed after lunch and Bruce collected me about 3.30. and we went up to Viceroy's house. The day was rather dull, but nothing could spoil the beauty of the gardens. There is a wide terrace that runs the length of the house, and from that stretch the very formal Mughal Gardens. Long narrow canal-like pools go the length and breadth of the garden. Where they cross each other are pink sandstone structures to represent lotus leaves with a fountain in the centre. Beautifully tailored trees like upside-down pudding basins on stalks and tall slender cypress trees give an architectural look to it all. Between the pools there are square beds of all white, red, pink or yellow flowers. Archways, pergolas, ornate carved walls and wide flights of steps all in pink stone go the length of one side of the garden. The pergolas and walls are covered with creepers and bougainvillea of many colours. Then comes the round garden – in the centre an enormous circular pond surrounded by a wide grass walk; then rising in several terraces the most beautiful herbaceous border you could possibly imagine. Designed I'm told by Peter Coats *(Controller VH)* We walked down to the swimming pool which is a short distance away. It is all white with a covered pillared walk round three sides. A row of fine jets of water on two sides throw out curved sprays over the pool. At one end are the changing rooms and a squash court, and at the other diving boards, and behind them a large lawn and flowerbeds full of canna lilies, and trees strung with lights.

I saw through all the staterooms – dining room, ballroom and the Durbar Hall where there is to be an Investiture next Saturday. It is an enormous circular room with two thrones, pillars round the sides and ornamental recesses in the ceiling. Bruce put on all the lighting. A huge chandelier sparkled in the centre and there was soft hidden lighting above the pillars. The doors leading outside are at the top of a broad sweep of steps leading down to the forecourt. From the top of the steps, where there is statue of George V, you can see all the way down the Vista to India Arch. A fine sight.

February 8th
Night duty. 0109 – Heard a plane overhead – Supremo taking off on Arakan tour. Joe Weld came rushing in at 0020 for final messages for him. Weren't any.

February 10th
… Picked up by Bruce at 1.15. went straight to V.H, had lunch under a tree in the garden just outside the ADC room. Simply wonderful – all those gorgeous flowers and the fountains playing – it was hot and lovely. Went for a walk and sat for ages in the round garden. Back to Travancore – where we lay in the sun and had tea. Bruce came back to collect me at 8 and we went out for dinner and danced, then out to see an old fort, how eerie it was – full moon shining through broken parts of the great doorway – jackals running silently about, you could see their black forms in the shadows, and dogs were barking in the distance …

February 12th
Night duty last night, a minor flap. *Mercury* had sent a signal from the Arakan which proved undecodable, called up Micky Hodges, who came roaring up, his overcoat over his pyjamas! And we set about it together. No luck. Sent a signal requesting a repeat. Back came a message 'just testing'. We could have killed them. *(Messages from Mercury were passed to us undecoded. We used an out of date Naval code, and all this was too much for Jasper).* Felt v tired this morning and would have done anything to put off going out – but don't like calling off at the last minute. Alex and Bachan – another of Auchinlek's ADC's – called for me about 8.30. Bachan is very amusing and awfully nice and had a charming Indian girl with him. He is only 20 and is married to a girl he has never seen – he thinks that is very funny. We went to the Rashanawi club for dinner and dance. The Auk and

Lady Auchinleck were supposed to be with us but were too tired after their tour. I was very tired and not a bit partyish – still I survived.

February 14th

On duty early ... Bruce phoned to ask if I was coming up this evening – followed by a note by a bearer whom I found hanging about outside my room! I collected those who were coming up with me to the cinema party, and we were called for at 7.45. There were huge fires in the reception rooms tonight – everything looked gorgeous as usual. Cecil Beaton was there, didn't think much of him, he posed quite a lot and was wearing an enormous mauve cravat. Didn't see much of Bruce – he was being v official with H.E. All presented again and then had supper. Chris, George, Bruce and self got in a huddle and were broken up to be social with others! Saw 'The Gentler Sex', both their Ex's came. After the film we had drinks and eventually left about 11.30, we were as usual about the last to go!

February 15th

Went shopping in the morning, got home in the nick of time to change and go on duty at one. Very quiet afternoon. Thought of a nice early bed. No such luck. Kay Oliver rang up to ask me to come and dine with Gene Markey. I hated the thought. However the whole thing turned out to be a wonderful party with very interesting people. We dined in the private dining room of the Imperial. The Maharaja of Jaipur was there, he is absolutely charming and very Europeanised having spent so much of his time in England playing polo. He is a captain in the LifeGuards and a Brigadier in the Indian Army, but prefers to wear the Life Guard's uniform! Gene is very amusing and in spite of his numerous marriages to the 'stars' – at the moment it is Heddy Lamarr – he is extraordinarily nice and a wonderful host. After dinner we all drove to George Merrill's house – FDR's personal Representative here in Delhi – a funny little man. We all made a rather noisy entrance and were guided into a room, and there I found the whole of Viceroy ADCerie. What fun it was. The lighting was all very dramatic, low glass tables lit from below, huge tinted mirrors – above the fireplace a sculpture lit from behind against a dark mirror – it was all very effective. Everyone played the fool. Hugh Euston in colossal form, Bruce in pretty good form as well. We took George and Bruce home. It was one of the most unusual and pleasant evenings ..

Little Hal and Jasper arrived back from the Arakan.

February 16th

... Night duty. Lovely evening so walked up to work – everyone rushing off to go to Hal's party. Micky in wonderful mood. Work pretty slack but bit of a flap over M.I's.and M.S. (Most Immediate and Most Secret) but it died down, didn't ring anyone up or get any one out of bed, though the D.O. and Army Group fussed a bit. Got a bit of zizz after checking and doing files. It rained during the night, the air was lovely and I could see all the lights over Delhi twinkling below ... Hal rang to say what a grand party they had had, – was a bit envious.

February 17th

Slept most of the day. Bruce came at about 4.30 and we had tea in the garden in the sun, it was heavenly just lazing and listening to the gramophone. He left about 6.30 but came back at 8 oclock and we drove up to Viceroy's House – we had a wonderful dinner in his room, how I love the scarlet liveried Khitmatgars who dance attendance on us. We sat in front of a huge fire and drank old brandy. In the corner of the room was a huge bank of white jasmine – I loved the whole evening – how pleasant it is to be quiet for a change. He leaves tomorrow with H.E. on tour to Madras and Central Provinces and will be away for a whole fortnight – he comes back on 2nd March.

February 18th

By Jove it thundered last night and rain came sparking through the window on to my face – it was hot and close enough yesterday for anything. It hailed and thundered this afternoon like nothing on earth – it cleared the air and everything was so fresh and lovely, but the roads are a mass of red mud. To 19 Akbar for dinner. Sir P entertaining an Indian lawyer – who, though educated in England, didn't pick up any of our table manners!! I have been asked to stay with them for 10 days. It would be wonderful to be with a family for a change, and they are such fun. Brucie leaves today to go on tour with HE. to Central Provinces and Madras. So I shall go and stay with the Spens'

February 19th

... On night duty. The day is almost done - I've suddenly become desperately homesick and depressed and I'd give anything to go home and see everyone ... I was very tired this morning – came on early morning duty and not much in the way of work. We played the fool a bit, but in this office that is not unusual. After lunch we had a mess meeting and decided to have a house warming party on the 23rd . . . I have been here for four months today – I'll never forget that arrival as long as I live – how lost we all felt as we had tea in our mucky state at Faridkot House . . .

February 22nd
Early duty things got busy just as I was going off. Got my things together after lunch. Amir did not turn up until nearly 4 o'clock, I gave him my case and cycled up to the Spens'. Lazed in the garden and had tea – just as I thought of changing, discovered that my case was not to be seen! – phoned the quarters and couldn't find Amir. Jumped on my bike got back and found Amir and case. Sally saved the situation by getting Jasper Vaughan to transport me, bike and case to 19 Akbar, pushed down some supper and off on night duty. Visit from MH – working madly when he came in! An N.O., whom I met in Ceylon, turned up during the night with a signal from Baroda – discovered that he was 'Cloak and Dagger'[1]

February 23rd
Walked back to 19 Akbar – it was a wonderful morning – fresh and cloudy. The walk did wonders. It was such a heavenly feeling to be at home after coming off night duty. Had a huge breakfast and retired to my very own bedroom. Got to bed about 10.15 after a bath and gorgeous potter round. Had the most wonderful sleep with perfect peace and quiet. It was raining when I came down for tea about 5 oclock and sat and chatted with Joan and Sheila Chapman-Mortimer who, with her baby daughter, is at present staying with the Spens'. I had to go back to the Mess to change for our house warming which we were giving there. I set off in the pouring rain. I arrived dripping, wearing Joan's pixie hood and old mac! Bathed and about to dress when I discovered that Amir had whisked away my uniform to the dry cleaners – there I was stuck in my pants, and no suit. In desperation I borrowed another – with two stripes, and became a 2nd Officer for the evening! The house warming was a great success. LMB came – beaming as usual, always remembering who you were and making us feel important – and Admirals Jerram and Miles, General Lushington and Gene Markey and all our own pals. Joan and Michael arrived very late, but we .had a very amusing time. All climbed into Hal's 'Mary' and had dinner in the Imperial Grill – ate too much – but it was a most enjoyable evening.

[1] Cloak and Dagger - this referred to those who dealt with agents in enemy territory

February 28th

Cycled up to work this morning – lovely bright sunny morning. The morning was quite busy, some flaps with old AVM Jones – it was really funny. Phoned Joan to say I'd not be in for lunch – which was as well as I wasn't relieved until nearly 1.30. Went to Mess for lunch. Met Margaret Maude who had just come back from Rampur where she and Arthur had been staying with the Maharaja. She had been given several fabulous saris by the Maharani. It must have been a wonderful experience. They took me back to Akbar Road. Had tea with Joan and then went for a walk with her and the children. Home, bathed, changed into uniform, had dinner and cycled up to go on night duty. A tremendous wind got up as I got to GHQ. It blew the dust up in great whirls – it was very hot. The thunder came later. Visit from Commander Linaweaver (US Navy – Signal Officer) who sat and yarned for an hour. Not much work as yet.

March 1st

Felt wonderful this morning – breakfast 9.15. sat about, then went to see the stables. Talked to Sheila and tried on her evening dress, which I must have copied. Cycled into town, on way back dropped into the Mess to collect some things. Back 12 – lunch – changed and back on duty. Quite busy afternoon – played the fool with Margaret. All sang hymn tunes for her wedding. Got invitation from General Stratemeyer, which I can't accept. Home – bathed and changed. Hal, John Sorby,– who is going home on Friday, lucky devil – and Yvne came with us to the Gymkhana where we made merry till 9.30. Dinner at home. Went up to give the minnow *(Joan's baby)* its feed. Hal bringing up his wind most professionally. Very tired – bed 12.15.

March 2nd

Up with the jolly old lark, and on duty. Wrote feverishly to mummy, under signals and anything I could find to hide it. MH, who was snooping around this morning, nearly caught me – probably saw it – still. Got it finished and censored, and ready to go back home with John Sorby. Sun beating in this morning and getting very hot. Bruce due back today from his tour with H.E. Early dinner and off to night duty. Wrote a note to welcome him back and to ask him to come to Akbar Road tomorrow, but no word yet, perhaps they haven't got back ... He eventually rang about 11– they had just got back, had a wonderful tour and they shot six tigers!!

March 3rd

Bruce came down to Akbar Road about 4 p.m. and we all went to see the Qutab Minar, and had tea in the shadow of the ruins. The tower has 375 steps to the top – it is an extraordinary building. There are stumps of old temples all round. We climbed to the top and had a wonderful view. After that we walked to the well where young locals jump about 50ft into 9ft of sulphur water, and are given 1 rupee a time – and boy, did they come streaming to do their jumps. Bruce has got my sunglasses, must remember to ask for them. He told me that some of the The Black Watch were coming on leave from Burma and were staying at Viceroy's House for a few day, and asked me dine on 7th.

March 5th

All the family up at the crack this morning. My last day with the Spens'. Joan and Michael went off at 7.45 – nearly took my hat and case with them – some kind servant had put them in their car! Cycled up to the office – heavenly morning. No one in GHQ, and no Michael Hodges, so took things to SC's office myself – went social rounds but few in. It is getting very hot and felt baked in my Blues. Back to the Mess. I am very sad at leaving the Spens', it's been so lovely staying with them. Amir, all smiles, unpacked my things. Changed in a hurry, had supper – I hate the Mess now – I've been spoilt, that's the trouble!! Back on night duty – black clouds behind GHQ and the Viceroy's house – with the evening sunlight on the pink stone it looked superb. A great storm broke at 7.30 and everything, dust, paper, etc whirled skywards from the courtyard and blew over everything – followed by rain, thunder and lightning. Bit of a flap in the office and informed that Flags would be waking me at 5.30 a.m. to collect everything for the SC *(he was going on tour to see General Stilwell [VinegarJoe] Commander Chinese Theatre).* – Drama – no sleep for me. M.H came up – and stayed! Bruce phoned me before that!! – fortunately!

March 6th

Up all last night until 5.30 this morning in company with MH struggling with programme from AOC – what a mess it was. Eventually he left. He phoned me later with the signal to send off. At 0611 hrs I heard SAC's plane overhead, we are now in for a very busy time and back to cyphers again! Very tired when I got back – had a bath and in bed by 10.30. Got up at 4p.m.and went into the garden to wait for Bruce, who came just after

4.30. It was very cool lying under the tree and we had a nice quiet tea –
Later we went down to Connaught Circle to do some shopping. There
were lots of Black Watch Jocks wandering about; it was wonderful to see
the familiar kilt and red hackle . . .

March 7th
Today has been one of the most wonderful days; I have been thrilled
beyond measure. I rose early after my long sleep and went into the town
with Sheila, hared round and did some shopping. Duty all afternoon –
screeds came in just before going off for poor Sally to send out. Bathed and
changed, a car called for Pooh Fullerton, Fay Ruthven *(two other 3/0 's)*
and myself at 7.45 to take us up to V.H. Bruce met us at the door . . .

Extract from letter to my mother
. . . " We were having drinks when a kilted figure came bouncing into the
room – Douglas Nicol – the last time I saw him was 1940. It was so heart-
warming to see them all dressed in the kilt. Bruce had everything so marvellously organised. He told me that we would have quite a walk before we
got to the dining room – he was right. Along the long marble passage and
up the wide staircase, we passed the State rooms, the vast halls were brilliantly lit and many mirrors reflected the lights. Outside the doors of the
State rooms are gilt chairs with red upholstery, which are occupied by servants when there is any great function. Halfway upstairs, one of the boys
said 'the piper will never find his way' – T H E P I P E R – I nearly died. –
Asked if we were truly having one and was told 'yes'. Was so excited I nearly lost the dignity I'd mustered to climb that regal staircase.
      We came to the room we were going to dine in – its glass doors were
open and standing outside were three of the fascinating Khitmatgars,
clothed in scarlet and gold and white gloved. They really look magnificent.
The room was huge. The walls were blue and gold, and a great chandelier
in the centre of the ceiling. There was a large bowl of flowers in the centre
of the table, and silver and glass sparkled. At the side of the room was a
table with wines and fruit – and khitmatgars standing in front of it, while
others dashed around serving us. We had an absolutely wonderful meal
and equally wonderful wine. It was all quite hilarious – most of us 'do you
remembering' and reminiscing. All knowing each other or each other's
friends. After coffee and liqueurs we had brandy, and just as that was being
passed round I heard the old familiar and thrilling droning up of the pipes
– my tummy turned over completely – and a red kilted figure marched in

playing 'Highland Laddie' – I could have wept with joy, and sadness at the same time. He changed to a slow march and continued round the table and then out and down the hall and the sound faded away. Back he came and once more round the table. He took his traditional dram from Brucie, saluted and marched off. We were all from home, but thousands of miles away, and all a the little homesick.

After dinner we all went to the Piccadilly, as Douglas wanted to see how his men were doing. We went up to speak to some of them, who were sitting at a table drinking, Douglas asked them how they were enjoying themselves 'Aw, fine sir but the only thing is we havenae ony partners' That was soon remedied – we danced with them – it was grand and they were so funny and amusing. – and oh to hear that lovely accent again. We gave some of them a lift back to the Viceroy's Leave Camp where they were staying –.and we sang 'I Belong to Glescae', and other suitable songs, all the way back. – It was a marvellous evening."

March 8th

Tired but happy this morning, last night will live in my memory for many a day. The work was pretty hectic this morning. Reams coming from Mercury, poor Sally was cross-eyed – almost. Everyone in their tropical kit except me! All looked very glam. The Supremo, Micky and Ronnie are sporting very smart uniforms of light fawn material instead of the usual naval white drill. Transport left without me – so I came home in a very luxurious car again!!

Duty again tonight. No loggers as they were all sick. Very busy but gosh I felt so tired and couldn't concentrate on figures – managed to get a cipher back to correct before sending it out. Busy all night. Brucie and Douglas phoned about 12.30 to arrange lunch tomorrow. They had just been entertaining the Jocks, bless their hearts. Thank God the Supremo comes back tomorrow. Can't cope with ciphers *and* DSO work *(LMB did not return. He injured his eye and was hospitalised. Arrived Delhi on 14th at 1845 during a storm. I was on duty.)*

March 9th

Transport left without me – again – I was mad and tired. Got home eventually in the bus with my Wrens. Bed at 10.15 and slept till 1230. Woke wondering where I was. Was collected by Bruce and Douglas at 1.15. Went down to the Imperial and sat on the terrace with a cool drink – it was a boiling day. Had a very happy lunch party in the Grill – Douglas is very

Part of the Mughal gardens leading to the swimming pool.

East Portico
Steps to the Durbar Hall

amusing. Went out to the station in Old Delhi to see some of the Jocks off
– it was grand to see so many kilts and red hackles –just like home! – what
happy days those were. It was so hot in the station and so dirty. Bodies
lying about, women and children, plus baggage, milled about – trains
crowded to capacity inside and hangers on outside, the carriages are open
to the elements, the dust inside must be ghastly. Food trolleys with highly
scented sweetmeats and spicy food, flies everywhere – it all looked so filthy.
We left at 4pm, and on the way back we nearly ran over an old man, who
was having a sit-down strike in the middle of the road – two policemen
lifted him away. Back to VH and the swimming pool. Hugh Euston
brought a hamper down and we had a picnic tea on the grass. It was so
peaceful. Douglas goes back to the jungle to night *(He was killed in
Burma shortly afterwards)* Back to the Mess. Our mosquito nets have
been put up, but I shan't bother to use it. Bed 9.15, after another truly
happy day.

March 10th
Another wonderful evening with my darlings. Duty all afternoon – quite
busy. Sally relieved me at 7 o,clock.

Extract from letter to my mother
'Got pool transport home, was in a bit of a panic as I had not much time
to get ready. Amir rushed round, ran my bath and all my things were ready
for me. It was an awful rush – but I made it! The car came to fetch me – it's
rather fun, as the drivers now know me and I feel rather smug – bad!

We swept through the arch in North Court, the chowkidars sprang into
life as the car drew up; one disappeared to warn the waiting ADC, while
another opened the car door. Bruce came out to meet me and escorted me
out to the terrace where we were to dine. It was a wonderful setting and
the night was so warm. At the far end of the terrace was a long table lit with
three large candelabra and beautiful flowers down the centre. Everything
softly lit, it was like a fairyland. In the corner, on a large carpet, were sofas
and chairs, and standard lamps here and there.

There were 17 of us, 6 of BW on leave from Burma, Bruce, myself,
ADC's and house party. We all sat and chatted while waiting for their Ex's
to appear. The table plan was passed round and I saw that I had been put
beside H.E'– oh lordy. – but happily I saw Bruce was next to me. Shortly
one of the ADC's said 'come on chaps, into line'. The house party stood
on one side and the guests on the other. Down the terrace, led by an ADC,

came their Ex's. After they had been taken down our line and we had all made our salaams, they turned towards the family and house party, the girls curtseyed together and the boys stood to attention and inclined their heads. Her Ex asked what we had all being doing today, and when that had been taken care of, she turned and went towards the table. After an appropriate pause I trotted and took my place, and we were all seated. H.E. is a poppet and it was quite easy to talk to him, I just prattled on. The only slightly alarming thing to start with was I was on his blind side and he would swing his head round in order to see you with his good eye.[1]

The setting, as you can imagine, was wonderful. The soft light on the polished table, the sparkling reflection on the nearby pools – and the deep, deep velvet blue of he night sky, high above us. The night was so warm – the heavy scent of the flowers filled the air. Everything round us faded from light into darkness. Some of the huge french windows threw out the light from inside, and the light caught things here and there – perhaps a tree which seemed to loom out of the darkness, or a corner of a pool, the water of a fountain, or patches of flowers. And always the marvellous chorus of the cicadas and bullfrogs.

There was a khitmatgar behind each chair, their scarlet and gold robes standing out brilliantly against the darkness behind them. Everything was timed to the second, the dishes served to each person at the same split second. It was a wonderful dinner party and though it may sound formal, it was not. It was really just a family party, remembering that Wavell is Black Watch as well. Before coffee was served H.E. rose to his feet and gave the toast 'The King Emperor' – that always gives me a thrill – and we all rose to our feet. We sat and chatted for a while, though the conversation eventually becomes a little distracted while waiting for their Ex's to rise. At last they did and we all stood back while they walked off down the terrace. I was just about to have a girlish giggle with Felicity when suddenly Her Ex turned round and came back. 'Good night children', she said, and took my hand, I dropped a curtsey – I must say I rather enjoy doing this! – The whole evening was so wonderful – I have been so very lucky.

We left to go to the Hunt Ball about 10.30. The high spot of the evening was when two pipers appeared. The floor was cleared and three sets did an eightsome. Our set had four kilted BW including Bruce, who partnered me. I had such a tremendous feeling of pride to be with them all. They all gave vent to the appropriate war whoops – the din was wonderful. All the

[1] Wavell lost his left eye at Ypres in the First World war

poor Sassenachs stood round and watched us barbaric Scots. It all ended too soon. I wanted to do a foursome but was sat on heavily by the more exhausted members of our party.'

March 11th

... Sat in the sun, and had tea with Bruce in the gardens, it was heavenly. Bruce has arranged a lunch party at the pool tomorrow, which should be wonderful. Dashed into uniform and came on duty – night duty again – it's very oppressive tonight – quite busy evening. Did two ciphers for S.C. and finally finished at 1145. There is an Old Wykehamist dinner at VH tonight; Wavell, Bruce and Arthur Leveson were all at Winchester, and a few more were gathered in. Bruce rang me to tell me it was a great success. They dined on the terrace, sang Dulce Domum, had the piper, drank champagne and all were a bit pixilated.

March 12th

Felt very bright and non-tired this morning got to bed by 10.30 and dozed until mid-day. It was very hot. The car came to collect Yvne and me at 1p.m. Arrived at North Court and were conducted to the pool by a Khitmatgar, where Bruce came out to meet us. The place was swarming with BW. There were three enormous red sun canopies, one where people were sitting and standing about, drinking, the two others were over the lunch table, which was laid for about twenty-four. We all had a swim, which was fun. The jets were spraying water almost to the centre of the pool – it was all very cooling. The sun was beating down on us, and it was a relief to get in the shade. We then still in our swim suits sat down to lunch. Afterwards some were going to watch a tennis match, so left with their Ex's, but Bruce, myself and some others lay on cushions under the sunshade and slept – with a few interruptions until 3.30 – it was heavenly. After that we put on the gramophone and raced about the grass – had our last swim, dressed and back to the ADC room for tea. The fountains were playing in the garden and the sun still brilliant made the water look like diamonds. Back to the Mess, bathed and changed and was collected at 7.30. There was a terrific electric storm huge flashes of lightening; all the huge Secretariat buildings and VH were lit up, it looked magnificent. Dined, home pretty late.

March 14th

Early duty. Up with the lark. Fairly slack morning. Spent afternoon with the Spens'. Later I went on night duty – the sky was looking very stormy. Just as I got to the office it broke with a dust storm, which whirled everything skywards. I shut the window. Doors rattled all over the building, and I heard things being swept along in the storm – great flashes of lightning – then suddenly the lights faded out. God it was eerie. Then the thunder started. I rang Bruce, I was so frightened. The lights had failed at VH as well – and indeed all over Delhi. Colonel Mann brought in candles. The lights eventually came on, but gave out a second time. The Supremo arrived back from Comilla about 0230 in the midst of the storm, he went straight back to Faridkot. Not a happy night!

March 17th

Early duty, not much doing. After lunch I went along to see Margaret, who gets married tomorrow. She was very calm and collected. She showed me her dress and all her things, they are lovely. Bruce called for me and we went out to Tughlagabad fort – fascinating place, a great walled town, now in ruins. Originally there was a lake round it. We looked over the edge of a wall, and below us was a small lake where bullocks were cooling themselves. Monkeys chattered and skimmed up and down the face of the walls. Nearby was a small Indian encampment – now and then a woman would walk down to the waterside with a pitcher on her head. Their saris were all the most beautiful earth colours, how graceful they were. Files of men and women would wend their way across the fields to their villages, the sounds of their voices floated up clearly. It was all very picturesque. In the distance was Delhi, and here and there the ruins of old cities. After a picnic tea we set off home again. Night duty was hectic. MH came back to help at 10pm and we worked flat out all night – 12 waxes[1] and a flap about General Gairdner's[2] signal which we could not get through as all communication lines were broken down with 14th Army. He was a perfect nuisance, but there was nothing that we could do about it. *(the battle of Imphal was taking place at this time – the offensive began on the 7th March).* Phoned 2914 *(ADC room at VH)* to tell Bruce not to phone as MH was about!

[1] Waxes – These were long telegrams typed on waxed paper that indented the typing. This was put on an inked duplicating machine and copies could be rolled off – they had to have distribution and 'For Action' put on them
[2] Gairdner, Lt General – The Prime Minister and Supremo's representative with General Stilwell

March 18th

After that hectic night,staggered home. Got a lift in Col Kohloss' *(USA, signal officer)* car and fell asleep on the way back. Got Amir to take some of Margaret's things over to Faridkot. Bathed and dozed for an hour, then up again and got ready to go to the wedding. It was a lovely day and very hot. Three of us got a tonga, went off to the church. Newsreels clicking everywhere – the church looked so beautiful – huge arrangements of white flowers and jasmine everywhere. Everyone was there, from the Wavells and the Auk down. Margaret was given away by LMB – she is so tall and so slim and looked gorgeous. She was wearing a soft silk dress made, I think, from a sari, flowers in her hair, and was carrying a huge bouquet of red roses and greenery As we left cars were streaming away. I came back with George Merrill in his very luxurious car. We swept up to Faridkot – Lady Wavell and advance party had arrived – people started crowding in. We had drinks in the hall and then wended our way towards the bride and bridegroom, both looked extraordinarily happy. Drinks were plentiful and strong! and everyone was in great form. Cameras clicked and there was general hubbub. LMB made a speech and so did Arthur. Eventually we left. Admiral Gounod brought us back. I rested! Bruce phoned about 5 and collected me about 8p.m. We went to have drinks in the Naval Wing at VH and then walked across to North Court. Poor old Hugh had got tired of waiting and started dinner. We had a very amusing dinner the three of us in Bruce's room, later having put the world in order we left to go to the Piccadilly, it was very hot, we danced, and got hotter, until about 1 a.m. It was a lovely evening.

March 20th

Night duty. An American Intelligence officer was Duty Officer, he came and talked for ages on interviewing p.o.w's in North Africa – very interesting. Bruce phoned – had a long talk. Gordon Blair is going home, will get him to take a letter ...

March 21st

Not bad night last night as regards sleep, managed to bunk down for a few hours – first time for ages ... Home and got to bed just after ten. Bruce, with our faithful driver Nana, picked me up at 1p.m. We went up to the House and then walked down to the pool. A khitmatgar brought our lunch in a basket and we sat on cushions by the pool and ate it. They even had hot pancakes and potatoes in their jackets – ham and salad. We bathed and raced round on the grass for exercise. I got very burnt and my face was like a lobster. Dinner in Brucie's room and home early.

March 23rd

On early – the morning passed quickly though not much doing. Got tags for my luggage for the great move to Celyon – how awful it seems to be going away, we have been so happy here ... bathed before coming on night duty. It started to rain again and the freshness was heavenly. Another terrific thunder storm broke and lightning flashes were striking right down into the courtyard ...

March 26th

Felt a bit tired this morning – not much work to do. Shattering news about Wingate – bit of a flap about a signal, but I think we coped. *(This was a signal confirming that Wingate had been killed in an air crash. This was Top Secret and Eyes Alone for S.C. However, it had been circulated round the HQ! Fortunately it was lunch time when I took over and I spent a little time running round every office and retrieving all the signals except S.C's – this was the only thing I did to earn my pay in the Wrens!)* Philip Mason asked me to have lunch – but I suddenly remembered that the Superintendent WRNS *(Dame Vera Laughton – Mathews)* had come from London and we all had to meet her after lunch. So I had to call it off – just as well, as I wasn't relieved until nearly 2p.m. Met the old Mother Wren, who seems extraordinarily nice. Went to my room, lay on my bed for a few minutes rest, and was so tired that I fell asleep and woke up at 4. Had a quick bath and cycled up to the Spens' – great black clouds gathering all round. Had tea and chatted. Sir P dragged me off to sign his new visitor's book. Home, changed and off to do night duty. The office again shaken by a V.R. chaprassi, in his scarlet and gold finery, arriving with a note for me from Bruce. *(another time one arrived carrying my tricorne hat filled with blossom, plonked it in my desk and pointed to it, I thanked him – he kept pointing to the hat – so I started removing the blossom, and there underneath was an egg and a note – 'cluck cluck' – it said, I dismissed him with a huge grin. I hated wearing hats and would leave them all over the place – this time in the ADC room where I had popped up for a nimbo pani and gingerbread cake, which used to appear for elevenses)*

March 27th

... It was cold and wet so retired to bed and slept. Wakened by WRNS Director doing her tour, and being shown all the rooms. Kept my eyes tight shut and they gave the tired watchkeeper a miss!! Got up at 4.30 and dressed at leisure. Went to fetch Bruce, who had come to have tea with me, from the clutches of the touring party! He was on duty in the evening so he left about seven. Admiral Miles wandering about looking for Kay, who was giving a party. Admiral Somerville was doing likewise. – Busy place this! Hebby came back, a bit pixilated and made me roar with laughter, and she sank into a chair in a dream. Did some packing and re-organising, and eventually after telling each other our life stories, got to bed after one.

March 28th

Bright and early – tra la. Heavenly day. Bruce called for me at 10, and we walked into town. Bank first then bought up the town. It was a grand feeling. The day was so warm and I am so happy. We met Simon *(Simon Astley, Joanie Wavell's husband and one of Wavell's ADC's)* and Archie John *(Wavell)* both on pleasure bent, in Asia Crafts. Finished up in Davico's and made pigs of ourselves on strawberries and cream. Went straight on duty. Colossal carpet removing by gangs of Indians. Home at 7.30 and changed. Admiral Jerram sent a car for us – the C.O.S's at that, which was so big you got lost in it. Lighting on the floor, and foot rack – luxurious is not the word. We arrived at Faridkot House and had a drink in the ADC room; the windows were wide open and great flashes of coloured lightning lit up the sky. It was a magnificent sight – the lightening seemed to be behind the clouds and threw them into brilliant and vivid shapes. We had a very amusing dinner party. Afterwards we went up onto the roof where LMB had a cinema. LMB, Joubert *(AVM and Deputy COS)* and General Feng Yee *(Head of Chinese Military Mission)* were already seated. The cinema is open to the sky and the whole place was lit up with blinding flashes. Awful film, "A Night to Remember" and by Jove it was! The rain started, but we escaped before it came down in torrents ...

March 29th

Up and off to early duty – felt wonderful. Not a very busy morning and spent half the time paying visits to friends. The whole place rather chaotic – everything stacked in crates ready to go – carpets up and everything a bit bare – but work goes on somehow. Went down and paid Hebby and Fizzy a visit and got some pay – jolly good. Managed to dodge LMB on the way out – got the remainder of his salute at the door! Bruce was waiting in the car and we went up to the House for lunch. The day turned out to be a lovely one, the sun was heavenly. Later we went down to the pool and bathed and sunbathed and came straight back on night duty. Was told that Micky Hodges was not arriving back until tomorrow – but lo, he turned up tonight – great alarums and excursions – he rang up, hopping mad – I sent a car out to fetch him. He arrived at the office at 10p.m. and turned out to be his usual smiling self – but judging from the crashes coming from his office next door, with safe doors slamming, was disturbed in mind!! Fortunately nothing exciting has been happening in his absence. Not much work.

March 31st
. . . Heard to my horror that all heavy baggage had to be ready by 0900 tomorrow, and I haven't done a blooming thing. Duty 1 p.m., very slack afternoon – went round chatting with all my pals. After dinner I went up and packed, got two trunks done. Yvne gave me something to help me fill them. Hebby came in and told me it was damned bad packing – ah well. Eventually got them all done and labelled.

April 1st
Early duty...Bruce collected me from the office and we went to pick up Hebby from Travancore. We had a hurried but lovely lunch by the pool. Mrs de Bath *(lady in waiting/sec to the Vicereine)* and Hugh Euston had it with us, and it was really very amusing. At 2.15 we rushed off to get Hebby back in time for her train, she was going with the first train party to Ceylon – later we went shopping and I collected my new white and silver evening dress from Georgina. *(the dressmaker)* Back to House and had a swim – then drinks in the ADC room. What a heavenly feeling to have 48 hrs leave before me. Dinner at the House, talked until after 11 then off to the Piccadilly and danced until 1a.m

April 3rd
LMB left this morning for Burma. A signal was sent ahead that he would like to talk to the troops and requested that he wanted only small groups at a time, and that a box should be available so that all could see him . . .

April 4th

... Didn't have much sleep. Bruce called for me; as usual I was late. We changed our plans and took a picnic lunch out instead of going up to the pool, as there was a crowded lunch party there. We went miles out into the jungle. The canal road was lovely – bullocks were watering themselves by the river and here and there people were doing likewise. As our car approached, parties of Indians who were in the middle of the narrow rutted track, scattered like frightened children. We passed through tiny villages with houses made of mud. Over a bridge and over bumpy tracks on to even rougher ground and into fields where we got stuck, and had to turn and come back. We drove towards Delhi and eventually stopped to have lunch under a tree, though trees and shade were hard to find. After lunch we lay in the shade, but had to get up pretty quickly when a herd of cows were being driven over us – more or less! As we were coming back through Chandi Chowk the driver said he'd take me to a shop where I could get some decent material. We stopped in the square and went up a narrow little staircase between two bazaar shops where I got some cotton. Later we picked up Michael and Joan and went to the Gymkhana. A lovely evening and most energetic – and it was *hot*. We danced an Old Fashioned Waltz until we streamed – it was heaven. A huge dinner in the Grill.

April 6th

... Just been told that I am now going to Ceylon on Monday 10th instead of Friday 14th, only four more days, I can't believe it. Broke the news to Michael and Joan – I'm going to miss them so much. Felt very queer all of a sudden – but all right later. Walked home with Bruce, took Simon's dog for a walk with us – lovely evening, the moon almost full. Went to Bikaner House for a final drink with Gordon and Tom then home. Bruce too late for dinner at the House, so we dined in the Mess.

April 7th

Last night of night duty in Delhi, I tidied up and made logs for next month – still can't believe I'm going on Monday...

April 8th

Didn't get to bed until 11 this morning after pottering around, and found it very difficult to get up in time. My watch was 10 minutes slow and I was late – again – oh dear! Bruce was waiting – we went straight up to the pool and had a picnic lunch under the sunshade. What a heavenly day – the sky was brilliant blue and cloudless. I sunbathed and we all had a swim. I dived off the high board, very badly – but a great achievement – I thought! Lay in the shade with our feet comfortably up on the table – God it was heaven and so peaceful – that was disturbed by 'God's gift to women' *(Peter Marriot, Captain of the Viceroy's Bodyguard. Very tall and very good looking, and did he know it! He eventually married the actress, Lois Maxwell,, who played Miss Moneypenny in the 007 films. He died in 1997)* appearing with a party. So we left and went back and had tea in the House. Afterwards we went up to see Delhi from the dome – what a fabulous view. The gardens looked even more beautiful from up there. The pools on the Vista glistening in the dying sunlight. Westwards stretches the Ridge and jungle. A gentle wind was blowing and the golden sunrays played over everything. Went back to the ADC room and played the Emperor concerto. Back to the Mess to get things organised for my farewell party. Ordered glasses and nimbu pani and got ready. Bruce arrived with the booze and mixed the most wizard rum cocktail. Hal arrived first and Joan and Co. arrived in wonderful form We drank busily until 9.30 then piled into two cars and went off to the Piccadilly. What a happy party it was. I got slightly pixilated – I think – still I was gloriously happy. Joan the angel asked Hal to take them home and left Bruce and me. We got lost. It was a wonderful moonlight night – eventually finished up at the House. I got home after 4a.m. I did some more packing before eventually getting to bed at 0530.

April 9th

It's not much good attempting to say anything of my heart and feelings of today. It was my last day in Delhi – 6 of the happiest months and great friendships – and I am going away from it all. Bruce has something that no one else has and there has been an unspoken understanding between us that has been more than wonderful. I have been so very very happy. I woke this morning after 3 hours sleep and was up by 9.30 – again a lovely morning. I cycled up to the Spens' and saw them all. We went to church together and Bruce joined us. How happy I am when he is near, and how I want him to be.

After, we all went back to 19 Akbar and had drinks on the verandah – goodbyes were said – and something stuck inside me – I could have wept. Oh God why do all the loveliest things have to end. Lady Spens was so sweet and said if I could come back on leave, to come and stay with them in Ranikhet where they went during the hot weather, and that they hoped that Bruce would come as well. Am I not lucky? The lump in my throat got bigger and bigger. Duty in the afternoon but I could not concentrate much on work. Bruce wrote me a note and he feels the same. Got Flo to relieve me early in order to go to Evensong. Bruce collected me and we walked to the church in the glorious evening light – how peaceful it all was. After the service we walked up to the House, while all the colours become diffused and magical. My last visit to V.H. We had a drink in the ADC room and played the Emperor Concerto once again. Outside the sun set and the trees grew black and silhouetted against the dark blue of the sky. We decided to have dinner before going to finish my packing, so we went through to his room where we dined, then sat and talked over a brandy. I didn't want to pack or go – Bruce insisted that he'd stay up and take me to the plane. We left at 10.30 to go back, and he came and sat in my room while I finished my packing – how depressed and sad we were. Got finished and he took my case out to the car on the stroke of mid-night. We drove back in the brilliant moonlight – the Vista looked mysterious. We finished our brandy and then walked round the gardens. They are quite magical by the strange cold light of the moon. The round garden with its huge pool looked magnificent – the great moon seemed to float in the water, and the flowers were shadowed blobs in the pale light. We wandered round until nearly 2.30 and then went back and snoozed until nearly 4.30. First we walked round to the great steps of the Durbar Hall, regally climbed them, said 'Hello' to George V and came down again. It is very sad saying goodbye to it all.

It was still dark when we left for the airport. We arrived to find the plane standing waiting – waiting to take me away 1500 miles from all my friends and Bruce. How strange and deserted the airport was- just that one plane – waiting. I had my luggage weighed – then we just walked around. No signs of the Wrens who were coming with me and no telephone working to find out what had happened. We were supposed to take off at 0515 and it was nearly that time – so we kept walking. I don't know which of us felt more lost. We did not speak much but were silently transmitting our agony to each other. I could not believe I was really going away. At last we heard that one carload of Wrens was on its way. We went and sat in the car and waited. All the Wrens arrived and gradually went plane-wards. I was the last to go aboard. We hugged silently and I turned and went up the steps. We took off as dawn was breaking.

Ceylon

April 10th

Arrived Ratmalana and was whisked up to Kandy. Delivered to the Queen's Hotel, which was familiar, as I had been there only three months ago. It seems even more Somerset Maughan-ish than ever. I have a very nice corner room on the second floor – two windows, which makes it very light. Edith (Hebby) Hebbler, who is on her way by train, will be my stable companion ...

April 13th

First day at work in new H.Q. It is strange and I feel very lost . . . Hal brought a letter from Brucie – he is as miserable as I am ...

April 14th

On duty and 8 a.m. The first thing I did was dust the place, it was thick – and proceeded to empty a pot of ink all over our nice new clean floor. I scatted round to get rid of this typical DSO sign and eventually Tubby got hold of the right man. The day was hot and sticky. Poor little Fielding *(one of our Wrens, who caught some fever)* died this morning. I feel so sad for her parents so far away. HH and MH [1] motored to Colombo for her funeral. Janey Lindsay [2] brought some lovely flowers for us from her garden – they smelt and looked so lovely. I toured round a bit to see everything – the gardens are gorgeous. All the paths to the offices are named after London and New York streets, so we can walk up 5th Ave. and down Whitehall – good fun. Motored back to Kandy with MH and Co in his jeep. Hot air and wind in our faces. After lunch lazed around and later had tea with Janey. Went for a walk round the lake the colours and scents are unbelievable. Met Admiral Jerram, who made us laugh as usual. Back just before the rains.

[1] HH and MH – Heather Hayes and Micky Hodges.
[2] Janey Lindsay – LMB's girl friend. Her husband Peter was there for a time, but invalided home – she stayed. Simon Elwes who was out in India and Ceylon doing portraits of all the famous, he also painted a lovely one of Janey.

April 16th

Up bright and early and felt it. The mornings are so lovely and the scenery so wonderful that I wanted to be out. We had an amusing morning – MH in grand form – he was very proud of himself as he had pinched a chair from LMB's office for us on night duty, it is low and gorgeously comfortable. Quite busy morning. How fantastic it seems to be working in these wonderful surroundings – tropical trees and flowers of the most exotic kind all round us . . . Some more of us have arrived; after their long long journey by train. General Wheeler[1] is back and was ensconced in his office today – he's so nice and friendly, rather like a favourite uncle – 'social rounds' are grand here – it's such a lovely walk. Was going to tea with Admiral Jerram but didn't. Night duty – the transport broke down – but I got a lift to the office. MH told me I looked like a chorus girl in my slacks! Tried to put a call through to Delhi – but what with thunderstorm and things the lines were down. I suppose 1500 miles is quite a long way. Very busy putting cupboards and files in order – people trotted in and out the whole evening. Found a Press Handout had never been sent out – awful panic – nearly got HH jailed. Everything turned out all right – had a pineapple – lovely. SAC arrived from Delhi today, they were all dining at VH on 14th and Bruce gave Arthur Leveson a letter for me which has just been delivered.

April 17th

I was so tired when I came off this morning. I had managed to get a short sleep from 6.30 – I just fell off in the chair! The transport left without me – I could have wept. But I did better in the shape of the Supremo's car, which was going back to KP[2] and got home in heavenly comfort. I ate a huge breakfast. The morning was lovely – blue sky and lovely cool breeze. When I woke I found Hebby my stable companion had arrived after her long train journey from Delhi – it was good to see her. The rains started but nothing daunted we went out wrapped in scarves and raincoats and went round the lake – The fresh clean smell of everything was a tonic – we sang at the top of our voices – we got home drenched – the natives we passed thought we were crackers, I think! Had drink with Pooh who has come by air and brought with her a letter from Bruce, dated 15th.

[1] General 'Spec Wheeler US Army – Deputy Chief of Staff.
[2] KP – King's Pavilion – LMB's house in Kandy

April 22nd

Early duty – had cold bath and went down to breakfast feeling exhilarated. When I got to the office the place was in an awful mess – sand and dust all over. However with the morning bright and sunny and the smell of flowers I didn't mind. I got a broom and started off. It was wrenched out of my hands by Commander Linaweaver who finished my dirty work for me. He also took me on part of my social rounds in his car – I finished then on a bicycle. It was very hot. This morning was busy as usual. Just before coming back on night duty the daily downpour started – eventually a kind officer got hold of an American truck to pick me up at the hotel door. The rain soon stopped and the sky became orange and pink and mist clinging to everything was tinged with the colours. Quite busy trying to make t/ps[1] route their signals properly. HH and MH turned up after midnight on way home from A2 camp opening night – He drank my passion fruit juice!

April 23rd

Not a wink of sleep last night. Every time I thought now for that lovely armchair more work came in. I was dizzy with tiredness when morning came I got our own transport back but was hopping mad with a chap who kept me waiting – to discover he was the person who got my transport for me last night! – He was quite charming.

April 24th

Up early and went down to breakfast in high spirits. It was rather a misty morning – went for a walk – the sun was shining from behind the veils of mist on the hill and all the colours appeared through them – steaming mist was rising from the lake. Got a cheery wave from General Wheeler on his way to Peradeniya. Duty 1p.m – flat out until 7.30 and dead beat. Just as I was going down for dinner, Hebby appeared and asked me to come and have drinks with Admiral Miles, and Admiral Geoffrey, who are going to the UK next week[2] I put on a rapid face and tottered down. Miles was in terrific form and it was really very amusing. We all had dinner together at 9p.m. Eventually got to bed at 10.30. It was a very pleasant evening but I was so pleased to get to bed.

April 25th

I felt so tired this morning – and did not like the idea of going on early

[1] T/p's – Teleprinter operators
[2] Admiral Miles was appointed Flag Admiral of the Western Mediterranean Fleet

duty – however it has to be done – the transport was very full this morning, and broke down half way – we felt it slowly dying on us. Fortunately we met one going back to Kandy and it turned round and picked us up. Too much to hand over for my liking and piles of waxes. Signals arrived from Delhi by air and a fat letter from Bruce. I was so busy that it lay unopened until nearly 11.30. Got a bike to do my rounds and nearly melted – I could have dropped with sheer tiredness today. After lunch did a spot of unpacking as my second tin trunk has arrived. On 7.30 night duty again. Fairly slack tonight and have almost cleared up. Visit from MH. Irving Asher[1] turned up – what a mess – poor chap crashed into the Persian Gulf and lost all the booty he was bringing from the US – George Cruikshank has 'had' his cine bulbs.

April 26th
... Walked round the lake this evening, the sun had disappeared but left its golden glow over the earth – the green of the trees was brilliant. A few Bhuddist priests in their orange robes were walking in line down the road. Sitting by the edge of the water in a wonderfully graceful group were some girls in bright saris of royal blue, orange and green – how colourful they looked sitting there, they have such beautiful carriage and bearing. I took a chance and popped into the Suisse to see if Hal had arrived. The place is stiff with red tabs and brass – but I suppose they have their uses! Found Hal who had just arrived and was bearing a letter[2] from Bruce – he's off on tour to Sikkim with H.E. on May 2nd. – had a drink and stayed for dinner, and chatted for hours. He walked me home to the Queen's. It was lovely – warm with a heavenly breeze. Lights were shining across the water and fireflies darting all over the place ... dashed off a letter to Bruce hoping it gets him before he departs.

April 29th
Not too tired this morning – in spite of working until 4.30 a.m. Hebby woke me just before lunch to say that Admirals Miles and Geoffrey were

[1] Irving Asher – USA Film unit SEAC, and a director in Hollywood " Irving Asher arrived back from the US this week having crashed in the Persian Gulf in a large C.53 aircraft. He was the only member of the party uninjured and had quite a task getting wounded men to the shore in their rubber dinghy at night. He lost some extremely valuable combat cameras and Leicas, which is a tragedy as they are irreplaceable." (LMB Diary 25/4/44)

[2] Letters – Hal Grant became our postman as he was constantly flying to and fro from Delhi in *Mercury* and would deliver and collect from Bruce.

leaving at 2.30 for U.K – but my letter wasn't ready for them to take – I thought they were going in the middle of next week – this *Overlord*[1] business is getting me down. Fell asleep again. Heather came up later having spent all afternoon lying in the gardens at King's Pavilion. Got dressed and went for a walk with her round the lake – it was heavenly, all the pink lights of the sunset over everything, and the water sparkling. General Wheeler caught us up and walked back with us – he's so sweet ...

The six months we were in Delhi were on the whole rather quiet. The H.Q. was now expanding enormously. For our office, more Duty signal officers and Wren typists, and our first lot of American WAC typists arrived who also dealt with the American signal traffic though they shared the office with our Wren typists.

We now had our own cypher office and the Americans had theirs next door. As well as dealing as before with London, Washington, 14th Army, Naval and Air Commands, extra traffic was now between Rear HQ and Kandy – this was prefixed 'Rear' and 'Kan', and numbered

May 1st

Felt so sleepy this morning. Not very busy. We have a new DSO – Susan Pearce – it will be heavenly when we are in 4 watches – I can hardly imagine it – three is a killer. Went my rounds – pinched some very amusing cartoons from COS's office about Wrens and took them on my rounds to amuse the cads. Home on transport with John Keswick[2] who was in tremendous form, battled our way through lunch. Later I retired to me room and lay starkers on my bed with the fan going overhead. Up at six and mucked around until dinner – there were ants all over the dining room table – but insects are all in the days work. Lovely drive to the office – pink misty clouds coming down over the mountains. Not busy. Very tired. Tubby rang me up as he was D.O. and I listened to his radio over the phone – like old times in Delhi when Bruce played records over the phone – from the ADC room when I was on night watch ... How I miss it.

[1] Overlord – Invasion of Europe
[2] John Keswick – Political Liaison Officer for Chinese Affairs was Tai Pan of Jardine Matheson Hong Kong

May 2nd

Managed to get snatches of sleep from 3.30 – 6.45 – that bloody little fellow Rousso *(an American from U.S. cypher office)* made a nuisance of himself, and I found it difficult to answer his numerous questions politely – got home just after 9a.m. Not so deadly sleepy today and got up at 3. Tea at Club. Douglas Wilson[1] wandered in looking for a book on monsoon floods – he's very amusing, we chatted for some time – then home and tried to cool myself off with a cold drink. The sky was lovely tonight – the hills with their tropical trees stood out so clearly against the night sky, and the lights twinkled from the houses on the hills.

May 3rd

Wakened this morning with the sound of the school children's daily chanting – it is such a haunting tune, I hope that I can always remember it. I also have the chanting from the Temple of the Tooth which is almost opposite one of our windows I have to say I find that rather annoying it's so monotonous. There is a magical Flower of the Forest tree just opposite the entrance of the hotel and if I lean out of my window I can see its canopy of brilliant red blossom. Colossal rush before lunch but made the transport. A letter from Bruce waiting for me in the office dated 1st, saying that he was off at the crack of dawn next day and not returning until 13th. Not very busy this afternoon – did my rounds as usual on my bike. I was very tempted on seeing Jack Clink's *(US Film Unit)* two doors open – so I cycled straight in, much to his amazement – was offered a cookie, which I accepted, – had a chat then cycled out at the other door. Felt in high spirits all afternoon. In the evening an American car came to collect us all to go to their mess. We had a few drinks and then in to the All American Dinner. There were about 30 of us. A huge cake was on the table and a little ebony elephant in front of each person – a nice gesture. The table was cluttered with stuff, from marmalade upwards! Jolly good meal all the same – iced tea and lemon to drink! I can think of better libations for dinner. Afterwards we all went up to Jacob's Folly[2] – a wonderful place. It is high above the stream which runs through Peradeniya gardens – open at all sides and lights twinkling all round – but by now I was deadly sleepy. Made a move to go at 11 and got home eventually at 11.45 – how heavenly bed is.

[1] Douglas Wilson – Air ADC to LMB, replaced by Hank Hanbury
[2] Jacob's Folly – Nightclub planned by Michael Jacob, who did the planning for the diversions for us all in Kandy

May 4th

We were busy this morning so I let Susan Pearce do the social rounds. Heather told me at lunchtime that I could go ahead with preparations for my leave – which is WONDERFUL – so if the monsoon allows it I will be flying back to India next month when the Supremo goes on tour. Incredible thought. This would not be possible if I worked for any other than these wonderful people who are sending me as one of SAC's very unofficial secretaries! On duty at 7 again, managed to avoid the small monsoon which was trying to start. MH not in a particularly good mood. Quite busy for some time. Meant to try and write some letters, but got too sleepy and though I could work – I couldn't use my mind for writing letters. Went over and saw the War Room which is an incredible place – the conference room particularly with the great map up ready for the start of *Overlord*, and others of the situation all over the world

May 5th

Didn't sleep very well. Got some fruit brought up and eventually got up with the intentions of going round to see Hal, but discovered he had gone down to Colombo – so didn't go – that was an easy decision! I should have gone for a walk – but I felt too tired, which was very lazy of me – still I will be more energetic when we are on four watches . . .

May 6th

. . . Afternoon duty – busy in the extreme only HH and myself there, and I enjoyed it – I love being busy. Told this morning that Moore the Telegraph correspondent was going home priority 'A' – and I want him to take a letter back for me but HH seemed a bit peevish. Romilly[1] turned up at Queen's this evening from Delhi and was going back tomorrow, he will take letters back for Bruce and the Spens' – they will now know my news, that I shall be back! He told me that the damage in Bombay[2] is terrific and still blazing . . . A rope has been strung round, on small posts, several yards from the Supremo's office. We think that this is to keep Sally at a distance – her rendering of songs from 'Oklahoma' the latest musical from the USA, seems to disturb SAC's meetings. Dear Sally, we all love it.

[1] Romilly – Colonel Romilly 'S' division (Cloak and Dagger 'Brigade') When I was back in Delhi, I took my little Dachshund on my rounds, once when I went into his office he said 'why don't you tell your dog to get off his knees' I was very cross!
[2] Bombay – An ammunition ship had exploded in the harbour on 14th April, doing immense damage

May 7th

Had to be wakened at 6.30 this morning as Florence wanted to catch the early train to Colombo. Got breakfast with a bit of difficulty – tottered into the car that had been organised to take me up to the office. Forgot it was Sunday and wondered why everyone was so late in the offices. Went my rounds – General Wheeler said he'd take me on as his PA!! Ho Ho. He really is such a lovely person. ML turned up later and we got very busy. Transport let Sally down – she arrived to take over in a car with boy friend[1] as I was struggling on the phone with Calcutta – it was very amusing. Boy Friend took Maggie and me back to King's Pavilion, and we had lunch on her verandah looking out over the hills. Back to Queen's for dinner – it must be a festival of sorts today, there were little oil lamps outside all the houses and the shrines with their niches were filled with tiny lamps flickering in the dark – it looked quite fairylike. Back to office for night duty.

May 8th

Had nearly 4 hours sleep last night, which was wizard. The little American 'Lootenant' was very amusing about my rest and didn't want to disturb me – he just piled the work up!! Had a nice cup of tea with the cypher boys. It was a wonderful morning I could have walked home I felt so energetic, but thought of all the 'bods' I'd meet – so went in the transport. Didn't get to bed till mid-day and was up again just after 4 p.m all ready to go for a walk – dark clouds were coming over the hills – but I thought I'd make it took my waterproof with me. It started when I'd got a couple of hundred yards round the lake – I had to come back – quick. Early night.

May 9th

This has been a wonderful day one way or another. Up at 7.15 – too early for breakfast so went for a walk up by the reservoir. It was such a gorgeous morning. Duty 1p.m. Fairly busy in spots we were all in a stupid mood. Rushed home, did some repair work on face and hair and we started off to General Feng Yee's[2] bungalow. Had some difficulty in finding the house. Found General Wheeler's car by the Suisse and we commandeered it. The party was a galaxy of fame. Everyone was in colossal form – noise all round was terrific – very potent cocktails handed round, liberally – very Chinese

[1] Boy Friend – General McConnel whom Sally eventually married. He became Secretary for Air to President Johnson
[2] General Feng Yee- Head of Chinese Military Mission

food – naturally. – The Chinese were sweet and tried hard to be chatty. We all had to sign our names in their book and John Keswick signed his in Chinese. Maggie breezed up to the wrong General to say good bye and thank you – very funny – but probably didn't matter in Chinese circles! We went back to King's Pavilion for dinner, which was hilarious, especially when Pownall[1] popped his head round the door of the bathroom off the ADC dining room, presumably a bedroom at some time, to see what was going on! Douglas Wilson was with us – he was going back to the U.K – and Hank Hanbury, who had just arrived to replace him we had a lovely time. Next door LMB was having a stiff party with Joubert[2], Pownall, Lushington[3] and Timberman[4] We had much more fun. Home at 10.30. Found Hal in the hotel lounge with a couple of pals, had a drink with them and so to bed.

May 10th

... Went to see Jack Clink and Irving Asher on my rounds. They had just received a quite unintelligible signal and we had some fun with them composing an even more unintelligible reply they should send back! Got shown round their dark rooms – fantastic. Jack has promised to give me some films to take on leave. Night duty again – was up all night but strangely enough felt very bright. Bit of a flap about some 'priorities' going astray – had Ross[5] and mail officer out of bed! They didn't like that much, however we cheered ourselves up having tea at 3.30 a.m, then at 7 again. Jolly good, I enjoyed it.

May 11th

Bed and dozed all day. Didn't want to go out much and intended to stay put. Hal came for a drink – we got deep into conversation – jumped into a couple of rickshaws and back to the Suisse. Hal mixed a heavenly old fash-

---

[1] Pownall – Lt. General Pownall C.O.S ,

[2] Joubert – Air Marshal Sir Philip Joubert de la Ferte Deputy COS (Information and Civil Affairs)

[3] Lushington – Major General Wildman-Lushington Royal Marines, Assistant Chief of Staff

[4] Timberman – Brigadier-General Timberman US Army, Head of US Commanding General's Liaison Staff

[5] Capt. Ross – Jack Ross ran the HQ Signals and Coding Dept. He was not part of our office. He disliked us and we disliked him. He thought it was his, not our job to put routeing instructions on signals that he had to code up and send out. He later became Labour Secretary of State for Scotland.

ioned and we drifted into dinner about 10p.m. Haven't talked so much for
ages. Left to go back about 11.30 – no rickshaws so we had to walk – I took
my shoes off and the feeling as I walked bare foot on warm ground was
delicious – the moon was full, the night still and warm. The lake was so still
it was like glass, everything a perfect reflection. The light of the odd car as
it swept round the lake edge lit up trunks of the trees. We sat for ages and
just watched, it all looked like some fairy scene.

May 12th

Was terribly tired this morning and for the first time since I left Delhi I had
breakfast in bed and dozed till 12 o'clock. On duty this afternoon – home
7 – had dinner and straight to bed. Wakened by Susan[1] about 10.30 in a flap
about a letter she had posted *(accepting her boyfriend's proposal!)* and
wanted me to retrieve it! She sat on my bed and talked for ages – poor kid
she was in an awful state. Hebby woke and murmured – 'So much for your
early night' – I couldn't have agreed more. Terrific shindig outside with
drunken BOR's. We decided there would be murder here.

May 13th

… Duty tonight was hilarious to say the least An American truck drove up
at 2 a.m.with refreshments for the American typists on duty – a can of boiling coffee, bread, chicken, peanut butter and much else and we had a picnic in the office. A 'cloak and dagger'[2] bod came with a message to send
out and there I was, helping the War Effort, with a loaf of bread, well muti-
lated, and chicken in pieces all over my desk – doling it round to all the girls
and boys. He was a little surprised! Well, some do work harder than others
don't they? Eventually bunked down on *the* chair at 3.30.

May 14th

After that hilarious night watch – and I did manage to get a few hours
sleep – but jolly grateful to get home. Met Pooh and Hebby who were off
to Sigiriya today … Strong minded and went for walk round the lake this

[1] Susan Pearce – Dear Sue was so worried that she might not be doing the right thing. She
eventually married him – sadly he ran off with a Russian artist about 35 years later
[2] Cloak and Dagger – this was the hush hush lot, Force 136 and SOE. For some reason most
of their communications went through the Post & Telegraph system, perhaps it was easier
by this system to tap out messages to the 'underground' chaps in the jungle. Their officers
at this end crept about in a most secretive way and ,made us laugh a bit. Once I hid a message under my blotter, and when one of their officers came to collect it, I pretended I
couldn't find it. Her anguish was fun to behold.

evening which did me a power of good. Talked to Susan while she had dinner and heard of terrific things passing through – the zero hour[1] is near – Oh God what next.

May 15th
… Had an amusing session with Hal this morning. MH was away and Hal was enjoying being SOIC for a few hours. Climbed out of our window and went across and climbed into his -'The Brits are odd' he said! His desk was completely bare – except for photos of his wife and children, but then we only took him seriously when he was driving *Mercury*. He had had a fantastic brooch of Air Force wings made with the centre piece – a swivel chair! 'Chairborne' he said 'that's me.' – God he's funny. Scatted round trying to get my letter to Bruce in the air bag. Tried too to get the low down from Joe Weld about SAC's Delhi visit, to discover when he was flying up – but he seemed to be going the wrong way! – but no doubt MH has everything fixed for me.

May 16th
The monsoon started in earnest today. It came down in sheets this morning – and tonight it was an incessant roar – and there was some lightning. I felt awful all morning – I thought I was going to pass gently out from tiredness – but I'm still here! We were all in a stupid mood today. Went my rounds on my bike – had a long chat with Jack Clink, and off again. Found DCOS[2] with his feet on the desk – working?!! Maggie asked me to go to lunch, but I felt rotten so said no, just as well as Susan didn't relieve me until 1.30. Home and retired to bed.

May 17th
One of the laziest days for a long time slept and dozed – didn't even go for a walk. Letter from Bruce who had a wonderful trip to Sikkim he wrote:

'… We had a great trip to Sikkim, and it was terrific to get up into the hills and be able to feel cold once in while. To get there we were more or less made history in more ways than one. To begin with we only took 15 hours, Delhi to Gangtok – no one has ever done it in a day before – and then our diverse mode of transport couldn't have been more different. Leaping out of a high-powered aircraft we leaped onto a collection of elephants, which

[1] Zero hour – invasion of Europe
[2] DCOS – Lt General Al Wedemeyer US Army

70

trumpeted loudly, bore us across a nearby river, which unfortunately was in flood. No one knew whether elephants could swim! It was eventually decided that even if they couldn't they might always cheat by having one foot on the bottom!

We then motored though tea plantations for miles and miles and eventually entered a large valley or gorge up which we motored in a tortuous, and in places precarious, road. This valley of the Tista river is so deep that although we were climbing constantly, it still remained muggy and hot, and the dust from our rather 'kutcha' cars was worse than the western desert. At last we started to get into the hill country and you could see the change of features of the local populace. They began to look more Asiatic and from the scraggy Indian, you began to see tough little men, with thick calves and cheerful Mongolian faces, clad very often in their one piece jerkin and kilt, with a huge kukri dangling from their belt. As it grew dark we passed through several villages and it was grand to smell the reek of a real good log fire again and to see the cosy log huts these people live in. We arrived in Gantok quite late at night and got our first sniff of mountain air. The people are so charming, always smiling and dress in gorgeous robes – some of them – and always seem pleased to see you.

Our stay was just like one long pantomime. We went to one official function which terminated with a cabaret show which C.B. Cochran would have found it hard to emulate. The Bhutan warriors were the highlight of the performance – these sturdy little Hillmen, dressed in a garb which must be something like the dress of the ancient Scots, perform wild leaps and turns in perfect time with one another, and with the grace of a trained ballet dancers. Their music is a bit painful – but rather adds to the riot of fun. Tibetan dancers did their stuff, and the local people – Lepchas – did a barn dance rushing round amongst some hay, which they had strewn on the ground, kneading it with their feet and yelling at one another to go faster, finally in a state of exhaustion they fall in a heap and call it a day. Finally the local schoolchildren sang Land of Hope and Glory which gave the party a more sober atmosphere – and we all went home...

We managed to get to the Tibetan frontier – 17000 ft – my, did my head ache. We made it on foot and ponies, but at one stage we almost had to carry the ponies! We reached the pass leading into Tibet in a roaring hailstorm – so feeling a bit browned off as they say, we found a small cave in which we took shelter. Someone produced a bottle of brandy and some tea and we had a rousing party, watched by some grinning Tibetans, who thought it was a great joke. It was lovely up there – the snow, rhododendrons, swift running stream and waterfall – I didn't want to come back, but one has to.'

May 19th
On early but with the wonderful feeling of no more double watches – I can scarcely believe it after all these months. Was asked if I'd any parcels to go home – and there in the SAC's office was a great bag full of them. 'Sister Anne' was being filled up and everything taken up to Delhi to go off Dashed round after lunch – bought dried fruit, tinned butter, tea and soap – and got everything ready and cycled in a downpour to the PCH to have it censored. Sgt Good picked it up for me. Hardly knew what to do with myself with 24 hrs off. Went to the sitting room – where I found a gramophone and piles of classical records. I wept with the joy of hearing good music – it makes me homesick and long for it all this to be over. I played Elisabeth Schumann singing Bist du Bei Mir and Ave Maria and a Mozart concerto. I remember in Delhi days when Brucie would give me a recital over the phone when I was on night watch – and I had a sick feeling inside and a longing to be back. Heard I'm travelling up on 24th June. Felt unlike dinner – played the gramophone until late and retired to my room. Just about to get into bed when a note arrived from Hal to go and join him in Gen. Beebe's[1] room – which I did as I was a bit depressed. Gen. Timberman was there – we had a drink and went down to dinner, back to Beebe's room where we played the gramophone – I danced to the 'Merry Widow' and after getting rid of surplus energy – felt so much better.

At this point I think I should explain why we were surrounded by so many Admirals, Generals and other high ranking officers in the Queen's Hotel by quoting out of LMB's diary:
"I am living with my personal staff at the King's Pavilion in Kandy. The most senior officers are living at the Suisse Hotel. Officers of Colonel's and Brigadier's rank are also living at the Suisse Hotel. Officers of Brigadier General's and Major General's ranks and officers of the Wrens, Wacs Cwacs[2] and women civil officers are living at the Queen's Hotel. We were all puzzled why Admiral Jerram had arranged the billeting in this manner, until a bright American officer pointed out that it was the presence of female officers at the Queen's that had made it

[1] Brig. General Beebe – US Army, Senior American Staff Officer
[2] WACS & CWACS – American and Canadian Female Army Officers.

undesirable to allow the young Colonels or very old officers now entering their second youth to be billeted in the same hotel. The Major Generals were considered to be belonging to the most staid level"

So there you go!

May 21st

... Off to Nuwara Eliya. Picked up Hal at Peradeniya, and six of us set off in rollicking form at 1.30. We had lunch en route in the car – as it was slashing with rain. The journey was magnificent. Great mountain waterfalls on either side of the road – terraces of the tea plantations – huge blossomed creepers falling from the trees. On looking down some of the valleys it was just like some of those model Japanese gardens, with the quaint tea plantation houses perched on the hillside, surrounded by clean cut terraces of pastel green and rich brown. In the distance the mist topped mountains towered up veined with torrents, some with a drop of a hundred feet or more. We passed close to many of them – the roar was terrific. We climbed a series of continual 'S' bends. It got cooler and more like Scotland. We climbed up to 6000ft – our ears were popping at one point. How lovely it all was – the change in climate and surroundings has to be seen to be believed. It was wonderful to be in the mountains again. They rose up sheer from the roadside and we could look down hundred of feet, with waterfalls gushing out again below the road. Nuwara Eliya is like the hills at home, and felt as if I were in Ballater again. Lots of lovely pine trees and broom in full bloom. Seeing a monkey run across the road was the only thing that reminded me where I was. The hotel was really rather like a large golf club, lots of panelling, rather dark, and sporting prints everywhere. It was cold and quite misty, so I felt very at home. On the way back I caught sight of some orchids – we stopped and I got out in the rain and picked some. When I got back into the car I looked down and found my legs were covered with leeches – I was horrified. Horrible slimy looking black things with their ends waving about – Ugh – Everyone shouted 'hold it' so I did – I was paralysed with horror anyway! They lit cigarettes and started to burn them off.

We had a gorgeous drive home as the world turned golden and yellow with the dying day. We went back to the Suisse and had a drink with Hal. God I was so tired my eyes just ached. We all went to the American mess for dinner. The rest stayed to see a film, but I couldn't make it. Hal sweetly brought me home and I fell asleep on the way. Went straight to bed – but I was so very glad that I went.

May 22nd

... Duty all afternoon. Informed on arrival that Gen. Stratemeyer had invited Sally and myself to dinner at Kings Pavilion – got home at seven and had to rush a bit but was ready by eight. Saw General Timberman on my way out and said goodbye – he goes tomorrow – I'm rather sorry. Arrived at KP a trifle late. Lord Louis was in terrific form, full of laughter and quick repartee – I think he must love parties. Generals Wheeler and Maddocks, also there. Dinner was most hilarious and grand fun. A huge punkah waved to and fro above the table, some wretched punkah wallah behind scenes pulling away. Two great staircases go up from the hall to meet and go as one up to the gallery where LMB has his cinema. After dinner we went up and sat in state with the house party in far too sleep-inducing armchairs. Not a very good film – still it was a lovely evening. Ronnie Brockman's parting shot was prize – he had fallen asleep during the film – and on the way downstairs he said 'well that was a very nice sleep Susan, you must come again!' Sally got a bit mixed up with handshakes as we left which caused much hilarious laughter.

May 24th

. . . Night duty – very unbusy. Had visit from MH and HH. Ronnie Brockman came in after 1a.m. having been working since 9pm – very amusing. Letter from Bruce, he is trying to arrange his leave to coincide with mine, I'm sure we'll manage although mine depends on when SAC goes up.

May 25th

Felt very bright about 7a.m. and had a quick walk round the gardens – it was heaven and so cool. I picked some gorgeous frangipani and came back to the office in time to put finishing touches to the handover notes. Lost the transport but got Sales[1] to take me home. Slept most of the day. Yvne and I were collected at 8p.m. and went up to KP, where we had an amusing dinner with Ronnie Brockman and Hank – H very rude about the frangipani in my hair! We had dinner in Ronnie's room and made a lot of noise. After dinner we saw *Jane Eyre* which wasn't very good. Ronnie was furious as the S C let some people take the chairs that had been kept for us.

---

[1] Sales – LMB's Marine Sgt driver

May 29th

... Hal and Co. back, and dear Noel[1] is still with us! – so signals are flying. Went my rounds and had a long chat with the film unit, as is my wont. Letter from Brucie telling me that poor old George has broken his arm - again! – only this time it was falling off his horse and not enemy action – and Douglas Nicol has been killed – oh God what a bloody war ...

Lay down after lunch – but an odd body from Trinco seems to have been offered my bed for the night and breezed in! Went for a walk and then gossiped with HH until 6.30, and off to night duty. A bit staggered this morning when Gen. Wheeler presented me with a box of chocolates.

May 31st

... An amusing story from Hank about Hal. Hal was dining at KP and as he was coming downstairs from the cinema SC pointed a finger at him saying "What's that?" Hal was wearing his chairborne brooch in his lapel!! – God he's mad ...

June 1st

... Reuter's correspondent came to say goodbye – he is going back to the UK. I managed to parcel up some things that I had just bought in NAFFI and write a hasty note – and put them in his clammy hand to take back with him and post them at home. Maggie asked YSC and me to have dinner at Snake Villa[2] with her and go over to KP to the flics afterwards. We crept into KP and kept out of sight of SC's elite party,[3] Uncle James[4] Noel Coward, Uncle Tom Cobley and all, and went up to the gallery. Pretty

[1] Noel Coward who had arrived on 28th, in a destroyer, from South Africa, he was to go on tour to entertain the troops in SEA
[2] Snake Villa – Maggie and Arthur Leveson's bungalow in the grounds of KP
[3] Party – Quote from LMB's diary of 1/6/44 – 'I must say to have Somerville together with Noel Coward was most amusing. They both have the gift of quick repartee and are used to being the centre of interest. They crossed tongues the whole evening; Somerville's opening thrust being quite unexpected. Noel had just announced that he had been out to Guy Garrod's bungalow to say goodbye when Somerville staggered him with 'That must have been a relief to Guy anyway'. Noel was not quite certain he had heard correctly until a second and ruder crack came from James, whereupon Noel replied 'Take care; you are dicing with death! I shall write a song about you'. From then on we never had a dull moment for the rest of the evening'. These verses were later written. (My diary 28/7/44) We were having drinks with the ADC's. when Noel came in flourishing the verse he had just written for Somerville and stayed for a while acting all the time. Eventually, nursemaided by Norman Ecforth, he left for bed.
[4] Uncle James – Admiral Sir James Somerville. C-in-C Eastern Fleet. Affectionately known as Uncle James. He was knighted twice, KBE then GCB. The second was given while at sea and a signal was flashed from a neighbouring battleship 'What, twice a knight at your age?'

gruesome propaganda of captured Nazi film, shots of concentration camps – ghastly. Afterwards we went to have a drink in Ronnie's room, Dougie and Hank joined us and it developed into a riotous party. Dougie behaved like a lunatic. Noel, our Noel gave a private recital to SC and we squeaked in our shoes to listen at the drawing room doors, which were open, then back to our party. Noel made some ruderies in the morning at the peculiar noises coming from Ronnie's room!

June 2nd
Duty early ... Tea with Hank at KP, he is amusing and I laughed a lot – It is so pleasant sitting out on the verandah, it is such a beautiful place – gorgeous gardens – the frangipani tree blew its scent across and the blossom lay scattered on the lawn. We played Oklahoma – the records were brought back from the USA – they are such lovely tunes. Johnny[1] and Ronnie joined us for a drink about 7 oclock. Home changed and back to KP with Liz Gibson[2] for dinner – it was a grand evening and we laughed until we could laugh no more – drank until nearly 10 and eventually had dinner – Hank shriekingly funny. On the lookout for SC, but he returned unbeknown to us and we disturbed him with noisy records till midnight! Gorgeous moonlight night – Ronnie took us home.

June 3rd
Early duty. Wonderful morning visiting all my friends in the gardens. Gen. Wedemeyer called to me that he had a message for me but as he'd heard that I'd since lost my heart he wouldn't give it to me! But he did – it was from my old friend Stratemeyer! ... Found Joe Weld sitting in state in the lounge at Queen's hotel – he informed me that the date of SAC's tour had been altered again – I give up. Night duty ... tried to phone Delhi, but whoever answered at the other end was quite unintelligible – probably the wrong number, happens all the time – dial same number five times and you get a different answer every time! – Hopeless!

June 4th
Cycled home – it was wonderful to feel the wind on my face. Passed all the staff cars on their way to Peradeniya which was fun. Felt weak about the knees at times – but it did me a power of good. Discovered at 4 o'clock that Yvne had gone sick – what a life – double watches again – still c'est la vie.

[1] Johnny – Johnny Papps. Controller of household to LMB. Before the war he was banqueting manager at the Dorchester Hotel in London, and went back after the war
[2] Liz Gibson – 2nd Officer WRNS – LMB's no. 2 secretary

June 6th V.E Day

Today is a day that will go down in history – we shall not forget it – or those who are doing, and have done, so much for us – We have invaded France – *Overlord* has begun after all these months of anxious waiting – Oh God that the cost will not be too great. All our thoughts and hearts are with you at home. Poor little England – how I long to be there. We heard it direct from England in MH's office. I wouldn't believe at first – but it was true ... Night duty – had to tear off without dinner – there was a terrific festival going on outside, three natives all painted up doing a belly dance at the hotel door – God what a row ... Very busy – all sorts of things flying. John de Lazlo phoned, he is down from Delhi for a few days.

June 8th

Colombo all day. Hank picked me up at 7.45 and we all met at the station. It's the first time I've been in a train since last October – getting very blasé about travelling by air and being whipped about without a ticket and neglected to get a ticket for the train. Joe Weld joined us at Peradeniya and we all breakfasted on the train, and a lovely one it was too. Lovely journey down with waterfalls at the side of the track. The heat got sticky as we went down. Saw lots of naked natives working in the flooded rice field and bullocks up to their necks in the river. Arrived in Colombo, went straight to the Galleface where we drank lots of nimbo pani, and saw some wonderful jewels on display. Made ourselves at home in Jerry's room – and all lunched together. Later we took rickshaws and went along the front. The waves were roaring in and sparkling in the sunlight. It was HOT. Had a cool bath and felt a different woman. Train back at 6.30. The sun was going down and sent a red glow over the water and rice fields. Delicious eggs and bacon on board the train. All rather tired after a long day in humid heat and sea air – but it was good after two months to see fresh fields. Hank met us at the station and took us back to KP for a drink and sandwiches.

June 9th

... John de Lazlo[1] took me up to Riverdale where Col Guise[2] lives. It is the most heavenly place – the house is perched right on the edge of the hillside, and looks out over the valley of thick tropical growth, tea, rubber and tobacco plantations terraces rise on rounded hills. In the distance the blue

---

[1] John de Lazlo was also Force 136 (his father was Phillip de Lazlo the portrait painter)
[2] Col Guise – Head of Force 136 dealt with agents dropped into Burma

mountains stand out with every imaginable light caressing them. The river with jungle to its banks winds in slow curves. We had drinks on the balcony. It was pitch dark and we sat and watched the fireflies darting about, and listened to music from London. After dinner we went back to the balcony – and there before us a sight such as I have rarely seen – the moon was up and gradually the tiers of hills took shape and light misty clouds drifted slowly across them. The moon was just above the trees in the garden and shone brilliantly through them. The sound of drums across the valley, the chorus of the cicadas and bullfrogs made it all very mysterious and romantic – it was all so still – no wind – just stillness. Col Guise is very Cloak and Dagger.

June 10th
... Night duty. Had to dash on duty without dinner. Sandwiches and coffee were sent out from KP. Very welcome and saved my life. Was invaded late by Ronnie, Yvne, Hank and Johnnie Papps absolutely no rest for the wicked.

June 11th
... Went up to KP for lunch – arrived at the gates, where there was a new sentry who stopped me – and I couldn't find my identity card. I marched up the drive with the sentry behind me – found Hank with room full of people drinking and pleaded assistance. Hank went out, the sentry arrived on the verandah, saluted smartly and said 'Are you satisfied sir?' Much mirth ...

June 13th
Duty all morning ... Up to KP for dinner with the cads – had a drink with Johnnie – we were all feeling full of the joys. Yvne and Ronnie waited for us upstairs, where we had a riotous dinner. SC having foursome downstairs, soft music playing for him through the cinema speakers. We all took our shoes off and danced very quietly in the gallery – it was heaven. Occasionally we looked over the balcony to see how things were going in the soft lights downstairs! It was like being naughty children, out of bed, watching while mummy and daddy were entertaining. We all giggled and stifled our laughter – quite mad – fun though.

June 14th
... Went for a run in the car with Hank. We tried to go beyond Riverdale,

but the road stopped. Drove by the river and across a suspension bridge – a gorgeous wind was blowing. – Climbed down on to the rocks – the river roared passed us – natives busy washing themselves rather perilously in the fast flowing water. Whisked back changed and back on duty by 7. They had been frantically busy all afternoon, and I spent quite a time clearing up. RVB, HH and YSC put in an appearance. The Americans produced newly baked cake and grapefruit juice for their Wacs about midnight – I enjoyed it too!

June 17th

Duty early. Lovely morning and all set to go to Colombo. Got driven home – changed. Ronnie arrived but Hank late as usual. Started off in high spirits and at high speed. Stopped for picnic lunch of cold chicken, eggs and tomatoes and pineapple. Natives stared at us and we giggled and stared back – we gave a little girl, who was chewing sugar cane, half a pineapple, and off we went again. We arrived just after 4.30 and drove along the front and saw the wonderful sight of the *Queen Elizabeth* going out of harbour, she looked so majestic in the sparkling water. Yvne and I had a luxurious room looking out to sea. We watched the *QE* and the *Renown* coming out with destroyers on exercise. A Sunderland patrolled and dived gracefully round the ships – it was a most inspiring sight. Then off to Mount Lavinia to bathe. The sea had huge spraying breakers which roared in, it was most exciting. The hotel is on a grass verge, fringed with palm trees, which juts out into the sea. The water was warm and wonderful, but Lord when we got out it was so hot and sticky. I definitely do not like humid heat. We sat on the terrace and had a cool drink, while the gold sun dropped behind the palms standing out so clearly against the water. The coastline and beach were turning pink as we drove back to the Galleface, while a yellow gold haze was spreading over the world.

When we left the hotel later it was quite dark, but on the horizon was there was still a band of light. A searchlight went up and sent out a bright beam on the broken water, turning the spray into a vivid blue. We all went to the Silver Fawn for dinner and afterwards Hank and I went out to Mount Lavinia and walked along the warm sands – how magnificent it was – the sky though moonless was bright and clear and such a deep blue that the stars seemed so much nearer, and so bright. The breakers roared as they ran up the shore and lines of phosphorescence glowed. Only the sound of the water roaring up and sighing back – magic.

June 18th

Raced off back to Kandy at 1130 – tearing off a door handle against a passing truck. Arrived hot and sticky in time for Arthur Leveson's birthday lunch. After a huge curry lunch[1] we all went up and made use of LMB's drawing room while Arthur played the piano. Hank dashed in and announced that SC had come back! – and there we were all lying about on sofas and on the floor – we suggested he came and joined us!! Later went on night duty...

June 22nd

Hebby went off to hospital this morning. – she nearly collapsed when she got up. Went with her to the hospital and had my foot *(it had been hurting some time with a sore under the nail)* seen to while I was there. It is a lovely bungalow full of sunshine and flowers. Night duty again and found that I had neglected to send a signal out on Tuesday – oh God – Cheered up by the thought that I now know for certain that I'm off on leave on 25th and will be back in Delhi on 26th – and Bruce.

June 24th

... Did lots of packing and rushed between downpours to NAAFI to collect booze and cigarettes, skipped lunch and went to hospital to see Hebby and took her some flowers – she has jaundice poor darling. I wasn't allowed to go in and see her, though I'm told Uncle James was! – Someone pulling rank!!?

---

[1] Ceylon was the only place I had curry the whole time I was out East – never in India, even when we visited Jaipur – the menus were always European.

Ranikhet

July 1944
Extracts from a letter to my mother
'I have so much to tell you, I hardly know where to begin! Life has been so full – so many things have happened. I can hardly believe it is now the end of July. I think that I'd better start from the beginning – that is just before I went on leave.

The excitement was terrific – the dates had been changed so often as LMB's dates were constantly being changed – I scarcely knew whether I was coming or going! I kept having to write to Bruce with 'no, it's not the 12th – it's the 18th, then not the 18th it's the 24th,' until I gave up and just sat back and waited. It all depended on *when* the Supremo decided to go on tour and all sorts of complications set in – all I could do was sit back and let things fly around me.

I was to go up in *Mercury*, the day before the Supremo, as far as Delhi, and work while he was there and then go on leave while he went elsewhere. Poor Bruce and the Spens'. how they put up with all the changing dates I don't know – it was more difficult for Bruce as he had to change his leave dates. To cut a long story short the date was finally fixed and I managed to get a letter off by hand to say I was arriving in *Mercury* at 17.15 on Monday 26th June. AT LAST!

We left by car on Sunday after lunch – Hank Hanbury, one of the ADC's was going on to Calcutta ahead of LMB to await their arrival, and was leaving the same morning as me, though in another aircraft, so he escorted me down to Colombo. The monsoon was going good and proper as we went down in sheets of seemingly solid water – we could hardly see ahead as the rain cascaded down the windscreen.

We arrived in Colombo about 5pm and went straight to the Galleface Hotel. Just as we drew up we saw little Hal sitting on the verandah having tea – so we went and joined forces for a cuppa. The heat – the damp heat – was awful, and I felt so limp and tired. Later I had a bath and revived somewhat. We had a drink with one or two people we knew, then all had dinner together.

I was wakened at 5.30am – it was pitch black and so hot – the roar of the sea through the open window sounded wonderful. I ordered breakfast to be brought up and promptly fell asleep again, and was rudely awakened by loud hammering on the door. Hank barged in to tell me we were taking off in three quarters of an hour – I jumped to it! We were bundled into a car and got to Ratmalana in time.

The two planes were all ready tuning up. Dawn was just breaking and the moisture was visibly rising off the ground – the sky was an orange colour tinged with yellow and pale blue. I was so tired I could hardly speak. I got my things put on the plane – blinked an eye as good morning to Hal, then sat in the car waiting.

Hank's plane, *Hapgift*, was to take off first. He was chatting to someone on the airfield – his plane had its engines turning – we gave him a yell – he came dashing to the car and drove it to the plane, jumped out and struggled to the plane door. The slipstream was terrific and everything within reach was being blown away – including me! He managed to throw his baggage to the fellows who were holding the door open by force – then ran back to car and back to the plane, this time armed with bottles of whisky and was hauled aboard with no little difficulty. The doors were closed and the plane started moving. They waved and then taxied off, and we were left doubled up with laughter.

I turned back towards *Mercury* and got in, and we were airborne by 7.30. I sat in the back amongst all the equipment and looked out to see the sun sending her golden shafts of light across the earth – and we left Colombo behind. I slept for about an hour, and then went and sat in the cockpit with Hal who has a very unusual way of navigating – he just looks out of the window with 'Ah, there goes Hyderabad' or 'Don't recognise that bit – must be off course' and so on. He tuned into London and got dance music, and we mimed a dance between us, and generally behaved like lunatics. Afterwards with earphones on and listening to music, I fell asleep again.

When we started to drop down near Delhi the heat became terrific. It was so exciting to see all the familiar sights again. We flew over it and circled round GHQ and Viceroy House. All the flowers and colours had gone – the earth was parched and dry and looked so different. As we started to land I looked out to see if I could see Bruce – we landed and I jumped out into an oven – the searing heat hit me in the face – it was 111 deg! A second later I spotted the crested VR car coming across the airfield. It drove right up to the plane and Brucie jumped out, looking so wonderful and handsome – he was in his kilt – it was quite heart stopping.

He told me that Joan was still in Delhi and wanted me to stay at 19 Akbar, so we drove to the Mess – now Jaipur House – to let them know I would not be clocking in there. It was wonderful to see Joan again. She had come down from Ranikhet a few days before to see Michael and escort Bruce and myself up. After hellos and hugs I dashed upstairs to change, then Bruce and I went up to V.H. where I saw all the boys – it was like coming home, even the chaprassis at the door remembered me and grinned all over as the car drew up in North court.

We went down to the pool about 7.30 and had a swim – it was heaven and so good to be back with them all. I was very tired after all that excitement – and the journey. We went back to the Spens' and had dinner and an early bed.

Next morning I was wakened at six to go riding – being the coolest time of day – we had a heavenly canter in Lodi gardens and then back for breakfast. About midday I tottered up to the office just to see how things were. How strange it was to be walking about GHQ again. LMB wasn't arriving until 4pm, so I went back to Akbar and rested on my bed – with a towel over my tummy and the fan directly above me going at top speed. Back into uniform again and back to GHQ – there was not much doing – but I showed the girls the form. The Conference Party was staying in luxury at Viceroy House and rang up to say how comfortable they were! About 5pm Bruce and I went down to Connaught Circle and did some rapid shopping. Later we had the most wonderful evening – drinks first in the ADC room and then down to the pool. The night was so warm and there was a wonderful moon. The pool was floodlit – the water was a pale aquamarine and the water jets at the sides sparkled in the light. The trees and the flowers, such that had survived the heat, were filled with strange shadows. The dinner table was on the lawn, and close by an electric fan to keep us cool. Dinner was served from a long serving table covered with a brilliant white cloth and with glistening silver – all this and soft light fading intothe darkness – magic. The pool is some way from the house, how such slick service is laid on is quite beyond me. We had iced soup, chicken and salad. Music was being played from a radiogram and we later danced on the lawn. It was truly wonderful – I wish I could find more adjectives! – and I never ceased to be thrilled by all these things I have been lucky enough to do.

Next day I was in the office most of the day. The Supremo popped for a visit to the office and as he left he grinned at me and said with a laugh 'I hope you enjoy yourself in Kashmir" – I wasn't going there – but at least he was aware that my coming up to work a couple of days was all a bit of an arrangement to get me to Delhi. *(For some reason the Eastern fleet Wrens were not allowed to go back to India and were, I was told, rather envious of us who could have it arranged)*

Had to go on duty at 7.30 the next day. I arrived at the same time as the Supremo, who again gave me a nice grin as I passed. Went and chatted with Ronnie Brockman, the Supremo's secretary. Hal appeared and after doing a bit of this and that went back with him to Akbar road. We couldn't find any transport so got a tonga to take us home – God, the heat of that afternoon. After lunch back to GHQ and sat most of the afternoon with Ronnie, making notes. It was very strange working there again – going up those huge impressive pink sandstone staircases and wide galleries with their ornate carved balustrades. I felt rather like a ghost at times and sometimes as if I had never left, and Kandy was some dream. However the bustle and the urgency were missing. I'm so happy to be back, even for a short time and thank God for those unbelievably happy months I spent here. Bruce came to collect me just after 5.30 and we went up to VH together, – it was just like the old days and I found it difficult to get it out of my mind – and had a drink in his room.

My toe, which had been hurting for some time, was still giving me trouble so Brucie got hold of Harold Williamson, who is the Viceroy's surgeon, to have a look at it. He said that he'd operate tomorrow. Brucie sent me home by car , as he had to be on duty. Back to 19 Akbar and found I'd just missed John de Lazlo – he had to go about his cloak and dagger business. Ready at 8.15, and Michael, Joan, Little Hal and myself all went off to Old Delhi to Maidens. John managed to deposit his 'secrets' somewhere and turned up, it was good seeing him again, and we had a very amusing dinner party – and it was cool – the coolest place in Delhi. Just after 11.30 Brucie walked in, the darling. Having finished his duties at the House he had come all the way out to Old Delhi, it was so good to see him. I went back with Bruce – it was so warm and there was such a wonderful moon, we stood up out of the sunroof and the hot air raced past us. When we came to the Vista we went flat out – the moonlight right in our faces. Everything looked very eerie, the strange heat haze making the buildings look ghostly.

Next morning Harold fixed up my foot and I felt much more comfortable. We left for Ranikhet at 4.30 Thursday 29th. Everything was wonderfully organised by Brucie who did it through the MSV's office at VH. Joan was in tremendous form and so were we for that matter, and the three of us behaved like lunatics the whole way up. We had to wait two hours in Muttra for our connection, so we had a picnic dinner, which we had brought with us, on the grass by the station. It was a very dirty, mucky place as all Indian stations are. Lots of little monkeys scampering about, rather over friendly, but very endearing. We opened one of our bottles of alcohol which we had brought with us and had a few drinks. By the time the train came we were all beautifully merry.

The train had started at Agra and Brucie had sent his bearer, Rhamet, down there with our bedding rolls, so that when we joined the train at Muttra our sleeping berths were all ready, linen sheets, pillows, loo paper in the loo. It was a large compartment with four berths and a bathroom. There are no corridors on the trains. We fell into our beds and slept soundly. At about 7am we stopped in Bareilly, and Rhamet produced breakfast from the station buffet, which he handed to us on trays through the window, and we had it in our dressings gowns sitting on our bunks.

We were still in the plains, the countryside flat and green, was so different from the dusty bareness of Delhi, – and it was still very hot. The mountains appeared in the distance and I started to get very excited. Soon they looked closer and bigger and everything got more and more green and we were surrounded by jungle. We arrived at Kathgodam about 11, where a car was waiting to take us up the mountain. The drive up was one of the most heavenly scenery it was possible to imagine. We drove up in a series of hairpin bends until we got through the pass and behind the first range of mountains, and then we truly were in it. The valley was now 3000ft below us and we were hemmed in by mountains – mountains covered with trees of every shade of green – bare mountains with terraced fields like great rounded staircases – great splashes of grey that were rocky landslides – cactus growing wild on the roadside, and in the distance I could see snow-clad peaks. Here and there the road had recently been cleared where a landslide, caused by heavy rain, had blocked the road. It was extraordinary to see the gradual disappearance of tropical growth and the increase of trees. There were huge pines, so much bigger and taller than those at home. It got colder as we climbed and the air was clear and fresh – the sun brilliant. We climbed through another pass and further into the mountains. The drop at one side of the road was sheer and rather frightening. We got up to 5000ft and then down to 3000ft, and started up again. This time up and up until my ears were popping. The stretch in front of us got longer – the valley before us seemed to go on for miles – and range upon range of mountains all round. It was wonderful climbing out of the narrow passes, I could not see the top of the mountains unless I bent right down to look up out of the car window. Then suddenly we were through the pass and there in front of us terrific grandeur, and there is no other word for it. We could see the road for miles ahead, winding up and up, and ahead and all round us peak after peak with sunshine and shadow playing round their summits.

The natives we saw were almost Mongolian, their Asiatic features so different from the Indian in the plains, and their dress was quite different. We arrived about 1.30. The sun streamed though the great pine trees which bordered both sides of the road. The bungalow, which was about 5 miles from Ranikhet, was perched on a little plateau and had a clear view in front right over the forest and the valley beyond. The 9000ft mountains were thickly wooded and full of the most wonderful shadows and shades of colour – and these were just the foothills. That evening the sky above them seemed to open and gradually snow covered peaks came into view. A bank of cloud filled with rose and gold from the setting sun, rested between the foothills and the towering peaks which seemed to hang in the sky suspended in space thousands of feet above the foothills. Little puffs of pink cloud floated across their summits against a background of ice blue sky, and great shafts of sunlight shone down on the valley below. One night when the moon was full, we sat out in the garden after dinner and gazed at the snow-covered peaks, which had come into view again. The moon seemed to be rolling on the edge of the foot hills, its light catching the tips of the trees,and Nanda Devi (23680 ft) stood out hard and white against the blue black sky – it was awe-inspiring and unforgettable.

We rode every day – it was like being a cowboy in the Rockies! There were not many places where we could canter, it was up steep rocky paths, and the horse had to pick its way very carefully when we were going downhill. In the village little boys took over our horses and wandered around after us while we shopped or whatever. As Ranikhet is a hill station everyone was on horseback – it must be fun to live there. We used to go to the pub about mid-day after our ride and have a beer – or two!

We were treated as part of the family and did just what we liked, I was so happy. We got up early and went for walks before breakfast, then rode, had lunch and then rested. Later we walked with Joan and children – home, bathed and changed into evening dress and either went out to a party or to the club to dance. If we were not going out we all got into our dressing gowns for dinner – all very relaxed.

On our last day we were up early, having been wakened by Rhamet who wanted to get our packing done – so I wandered through to Joan's room to pass the time, when Lady Spens called to come quickly as the snows were in view again. We all rushed to the garden – there we could see the whole panorama – the wreaths of cloud had lifted from the foothills and the whole majestic sweep was in view, and the clear bright sun lit the world. We clambered up the slope behind the house to watch. After breakfast we went for our last walk. We climbed up to the great flat over-hanging rock half way up the hill and had a world of pine trees and shaded valley before us and we lay in the sun exalting in what we had seen. We wanted to remember this moment, so Brucie set the camera and rushed to be beside me so's he could be in the shot as well. *(since know as the Woodland Idyll)* We left at 2pm sharp and we had not gone far before it started to rain, it came down in torrents and there was mist all round us. We arrived at Kathgodam at 5.15 and went into the station for a cup of tea. A half hearted punkah wallah was trying to keep us cool. We eventually left about 7pm. The sunset on the flat plains was like a glowing fire flashing though the trees. We arrived at Bareilly at 10.30 and sat on our luggage – and got pixilated on gin – with all the strange noises, and Indians lying around, or sitting on their hunkers, chatting away. A huge tree sheltered us, and flame lamps lit the station. We entrained at 12.30. All bedding arranged and in place by Rhamet, as usual. There were no lights in the loo and it was rather smelly – we coped.

I was more than sad to leave, I had forgotten about work, Kandy and all at SACSEA, in fact to use a South East Asia expression 'I couldn't have cared less' what happened to it.

On returning to Delhi, I found a signal had been sent to say that I had to return to Colombo in *Sister Anne* – LMB's short haul plane. Dawn was just breaking as I got to the airport at 5.30. Sister Anne was waiting on the runway in the glare of the flares – the Captain met me and gave me a note from Hank, saying that he had briefed him to look after me! I was standing chatting to the pilot just before we were getting ready to take off, when a Viceregal car came rushing up – and my Brucie hopped out. I was so happy that he had come and it was with a lightened heart that I left, as I knew he was coming down to Ceylon next month. Last time I left Delhi I thought I might never see him again. He stood on the runway as we took off.

I must say I felt pretty smug, as I was the only passenger aboard, knowing that its return to Ceylon was delayed on my behalf! It is the last word in comfort: two divan beds, four well-spaced comfortable seats and a table, with individual fans on the walls above the beds and chairs – bathroom and kitchen. I was given orange juice and coffee and later served with lunch – what enormous luxury.

I slept most of the way on one of the comfy beds – met some pretty rough weather round about Bangalore, which we circled round and eventually landed – had a cup of coffee and were off again. I was met at Ratmalana by Hank. I stayed the night at the Galleface, and was motored up the next day. Strange being back – leave seemed like a wonderful dream. The consolation is that everyone is so nice to come back to.'

Last days in Ceylon

July 13th

Back on duty after a wonderful leave – it is an odd feeling, but it is very nice to see them all again and it seems such a long time since I left – into another world. Heard the wonderful story of Irene Richardson's attempt to set fire to SAC's office[1] She had put all the official photos in her filing cabinet. Hung a lit bulb inside hopefully to keep them from getting damp. There was an amusing description about it in our office diary *(see also' July 4th' in Yvne's 'Natty Notes')* There was not a great deal to do except read what and what not to do. Went back to Snake Villa with Maggie for lunch. We sat on the verandah looking out on to the hills – very peaceful.

July 14th

This has been a most exciting day. On duty p.m. The afternoon was very quiet – HH not in one of her better moods – found quite a lot to scat around and do – chatted to various people and so the afternoon passed. Collected by Hank in his jeep and roared home. Arrived with my hair on end and tried to change and look presentable in 20 minutes – almost! Ronnie Brockman called for us with the Cadillac – better than open jeep when all dressed up! – and glided us up to KP. We were the first to arrive. ML and AL[2] arrived, then Peter Murphy[3] made his appearance, followed

---

[1] From Mountbatten Diary 5/7/44 'The Flag Lieutenant has a new assistant, Third Officer Irene Richardson, who has been transferred from my Secretary's office. Being an extremely efficient and enthusiastic person she set about getting Flags' files in order. She collected a list of all the people who had been to lunch and dinner and all the social letters that had been written and all the photographs that were waiting despatch home and put them in a new filing cabinet in the bottom of which she placed a powerful electric bulb so as to keep the photographs and files dry. On the night of July 4th there were great Independance Day celebrations going on in the American camp when an American military policeman rang up the Officer's Mess and said there was a fire in my office! Irving Asher took the message and collected a party to go down. They arrived to find my office on fire as the bulb had been left on in the filing cabinet. The local fire engine had been sent for but was held up by the sentry at the gate while every member of the Fire Brigade had to show his identity card! Although most of the papers were burnt, curiously enough photographs were mostly only singed. Miss Richardson who is known to her friends as 'the amiable horse', was heartbroken at this poor reward that Fate had bestowed on her zeal!'

[2] ML & A.L.– Maggie and Arthur Leveson

[3] Peter Murphy: He was in SEA Command as odd job man to Mountbatten: he played the piano beautifully and was extremely amusing. I'm told he wrote SC's speeches

by the Supremo. It was all very informal and great fun. Janey, Yvne, Maggie and myself, the Supremo, Peter Murphy, Arthur, Hank, Ronnie and Johnnie made up the party. We had a hilarious dinner and afterwards sat and talked while music drifted down from the balcony. Later we all sat round a table and played a drawing game, rather like chinese whispers. Lord Louis started by copying a bit from a drawing, which was screened from view – I copied and the next person copied from me and so on. The results were fantastic. It started as we later saw from quite a small subject and finished at the other end on several sheets of paper. Highly amusing and ML and I were quite weak with laughter. We then went up to the gallery and danced – LMB hauled me round – he dances very well! I broke the party up as I had to be on duty at midnight. H took me back to the Queen's – changed, packed something to change into in the morning as we were all going down to Colombo on the early train.

July 15th
My birthday today – how quickly these last few years have passed, and how strange it all seems. Donald was wounded in Sicily a year ago today, and died two days later. Changed out of my slacks in the other office and was collected and off to the station – it was a lovely bright clear morning. We had breakfast on the train. I felt myself getting more and more tired, eventually I curled up on the seat and fell asleep, and woke just before arriving in Colombo. There was a car waiting for us and we went straight to the Galleface. Met Mollie Baugh sunning herself on the balcony. We had a nimbo pani and then went for a walk along the front – the sun and wind were terrific. Got back and retired to the bar for a drink – trying hard to keep awake. Retired up to my room – ordered a sandwich lunch, bathed and curled up in bed. YSC and Ronnie turned up noisily at 5.30. Had a cuppa and we all went out to Mount Lavinia just as the sun was setting behind the palm trees. Later we went to the Silver Fawn for dinner, and back to Mount Lavinia – the sea was well in – we walked bare footed along the warm sands then for fun walked right into the sea fully clothed!!

July 16th
Not a very early start – a car drove us down to the jetty where we embarked on a barge and were taken out to HMS *Phoebe*. The water sparkled and great waves sprayed over the breakwater. It was a wonderful thrill to be aboard a ship again. We had a drink in the Admiral's cabin and after visiting the wardroom, back to his cabin for lunch. We were then

taken round the cruiser. – The *Victorious* and *Indomitable* were alongside – they looked superb. It was heaven standing on the bridge and looking at those majestic ships around us. After tea on board we left about 4.30. There was a bit of a flap about *Hapgift*.[1] Train back to Kandy and back on duty at midnight – what again. Lovely long letter from Brucie he is back up in Simla.

July 17th
What a night – I was dead by eight a.m. and then found a mess had been made of the *Hapgift* signal and rushed round and got it straight – I hope. Left for home just after 9 – got to bed just after 11 and slept on and off until nearly 7. Phone call from Hal to say that General Stratemeyer had turned up and would I dine with them. Had drinks in Gen. Beebe's room – Strat in grand form, we all had dinner together – danced a bit and I left at 11.

July 19th
All the C in C's have arrived for discussions[2] and the place is hotching with brass. Carton de Wiart arrived today from Chungking.

July 20th
Came off duty midnight last night and woke feeling awful – stayed in bed all day, dozing. Was rudely hauled out of bed in the afternoon to come up to the office about the routeing of the *Hapgift* signal, which was sent to Chungking but seemed to have gone half way round the world to get there – oh dear. However MH was sweet about it all, and after all Carton de Wiart did arrive! I wandered about feeling rather ill – sat and chatted with Maggie and Susan and eventually got home at about 7 with HH and MH. Changed and went with Irene Richardson to the Suisse. The place was crowded. All the C in C's were there. Al Wedemeyer in tremendous form as usual. It was a wonderfully organized party and most gorgeous food. Back to duty at midnight. Everyone seems to be working late after the momentous meeting today. Entertained Philip Mason[3] and his successor in the office. Came home in ACOS's car and could lie back and zizz.

[1] *Hapgift*, one of Mountbatten's planes which had been sent to pick up General Carton de Wiart from Chungking for the discussions to be held in Kandy the following week
[2] Discussions, these were about two plans, firstly for aborting DRACULA – an amphibious assault on Rangoon, and CAPITAL, the advance by 14th Army on Mandalay
[3] Philip Mason, Director of Plans SEA Command. He was in the Colonial Service in India and has written many books on India under his own name and as Philip Woodruff – also A Tribute to the Signal Office, see Natty Notes

July 22nd

Pottered until lunchtime . . . Came on duty after lunch and was greeted with several bombshells. Florence and Susan Pierce are both down with dengue *(a tropical fever spread by mosquitoes)* – so YSC, Maggie and self are the sole supporters. Very little to do and was so pleased when Margaret arrived at 7. Went home in the Supremo's car and amused myself with all the gadgets, the only thing I wanted was the covers to come off the pennants so that I could have them fluttering on the bonnet just for me, but Sales didn't think that was a good idea! Went up to KP to have dinner with the ADC's but didn't dine until nearly 10, as there was a continual stream of visitors to see the Supremo and the ADC's were dashing about. First of all Irving Asher then John Keswick and others and finally the arrival of dear Noel from one of his performances.

July 23rd

. . . HH phoned to arrange picking me up to have lunch with Philip Mason. Went down to the hotel lounge where I found Mike Umfreville[1] boiling up with rage with Noel Coward, he said it was like being a nursemaid to a naughty temperamental child whom he couldn't spank! Sat with Tru. Joe and Babs until the car arrived. Philip's bungalow is lovely and he mixes a very good cocktail. We had a hot curry lunch. Back to KP where everything is upside down in preparation for our Noel. We heard Noel and LMB talking rather loudly – I took my leave quietly! Changed and came on duty. Met RVB and YSC just going off duty to join the merry party at KP. Letter from Brucie. Listened to Noel through the phone by carefully arranged plan.

Extract from letter to my mother

'The latest thrill was the visit by Noel Coward. He was staying with the Supremo, and gave a performance in Kandy and another at King's Pavilion. Unfortunately I was on night duty the night he was performing at KP, however everything was organised and under control. The performance was to be held in the hall at KP in the well of the staircases which lead up to the gallery – the handset of a nearby telephone was to be lifted off just before the performance began. The naval operator at the exchange at KP was alerted – he rang me at 9.30 'The receiver has been lifted off. Shall I connect you ma'am?' I had to laugh. I heard the whole perform

[1] Mike Umfreville, was formerly ADC to LMB and was sent as conducting officer to Noel while he was on tour

ance – I told one of my wrens to pick up the extension, and we sat for one and half-hours with the phone glued to our ears. I told the exchange to put all incoming calls through on the other phone. Anyone who came into the office was greeted with 'sssh'. At the end I heard the receiver being replaced.

Next night I dined at KP with the ADC's and Norman Hackforth,[1] who was very amused when he heard how I'd heard the performance. Evidently they had fixed the receiver to the banisters above the piano and put someone to look after it!! Next night we met the great man himself. We were having drinks after dinner with the ADC's when he came bursting into the room – 'I must find Dickie – where is Dickie?' he said dramatically flourishing verses that he had just rapidly composed for Admiral Somerville. He stayed with us for a while – then shook us all warmly by the hand, said goodnight, and departed as dramatically as he had arrived! I don't think I like him very much he's so full of himself.' *(see footnote diary 1/6/44)*

July 29th
Almost slept in . . . Early duty- found plenty to do chuntering round chattering to everyone – the place is busy preparing for LMB's visit to the UK next week – all papers being done up in steel boxes and people buzzing round. It's staggering to think they will only take 48 hours to get there – have to get busy to get letters and any parcels ready to go back in the *York (LMB's long haul plane)*. All my photos arrived with a letter from Brucie this morning – it's wonderful to have them. What a glorious leave that was, and how very lucky I am . . . LMB up in the hills at Dimbula, so all is quiet. Tea at KP with Johnnie, afterwards he took me back to Queen's and then up to Peradeniya for night duty. Sandwiches eggs and tea arrived for me from KP at 1030 – lovely – and I was so hungry. MH and HH appeared at 0300. It was quite thrilling to think that they were going home with LMB. Saw them off in their car. I was sad that SAC was taking all my playmates with him. We shall probably be very busy all the same with masses of signals from the U.K.

July 31st
. . . Bought lots of things to send home as Johnnie said that I could send a parcel of about 7 lbs to go back to U.K. on *Sister Anne*. On duty p.m.

[1] Norman Hackforth, Noel's accompanist and companion whilst on tour.

Everybody very busy. Left at 7 leaving SC's office and planners up to their necks in work. Up to KP for drinks. General Stilwell[1] has arrived. He went straight to his bungalow. SC came back at about 10. Johnnie came bursting in, furious, and put away two cocktails very quickly. Everyone getting very fraught. We couldn't be bothered seeing the film and sat down to supper at 10 p.m. Everyone is getting very excited and worked up about the imminent departure of SAC & Co. to the UK.

August 1st
Thank God they have changed the watch and I don't have to go on until this afternoon. Took my parcel up to KP where Moore[2] got me packing and string. Came on duty at 1. Everyone in a state of chaos. Met Johnnie – asked him if he'd got my parcel he replied 'Yes it was 7lbs weighing 20 !!' Ah well. Back to KP – all the baggage was there ready for weighing. We had a drink with Johnnie, Joe and Tru – helped to address some labels for H's luggage. Maggie and Arthur appeared. We had dinner – Johnnie appeared again we chatted for a while then he had to rush off. Everything was rush, rush, rush. Hank walked me home just after 11 – the night was calm with brilliant moonlight, and the lake was still. We sat and talked by the lake. Said goodbye – and I asked him to give my love to England.

August 2nd
... A bit depressed at the thought of the exitus, there will be no dramas, no bustle or hectic comings and going. Morning duty ... YSC came up early to get the last minute signals. Dashed over to say goodbye to Joe Weld, who was all ready to go. The place already seems empty. They all got off safely at 12.30 ...

August 3rd
... Lazy day. Up to Peradeniya, collected YSC, ML and Sally and we all went to Jacob's Folly for a huge lunch. It was lovely sitting looking out on the river – a heavenly breeze was blowing right through the dining room. In the evening Johnnie collected YSC and me to go the cocktail party for General Stillwell – a lot of people there. He is a strange looking man with hair en brosse and steel rimmed glasses, he hadn't much to say for himself

---

[1] General Stilwell, US Army. Northern Area Command and Deputy Supreme Commander – he came to Kandy whilst LMB was in the UK
[2] Moore LMB's Petty Officer steward

– he has been well named Vinegar Joe ! – though his Pilot and ADC were quite amusing. Back KP for dinner – on duty at midnight

August 5th
. . . Sped on duty p.m. Not too much doing. The place is rather like a morgue without all the bustle. No social rounds – no one here. Now I know what Brucie felt when the HQ moved from Delhi. The ETA for LMB's party arrived – they were due at Northholt at 2030 BST 4th Aug. Back – had a drink with Hal – early bed

August 6th
Early duty, Sunday – no one in and all on my own. Stilwell created a fuss over security on a signal received from SAC about his tour programme!! . .

August 8th
. . . Very busy last night. LOKAN's[1] kept pouring in until I was sick of them – had to ring General Lamplough *(Director of Intelligence)* at 0130 to tell him he had to go back to the UK to join the 'party' Had dinner with Hal and we put the world right. Bed early.

August 9th
Woke very early and felt wonderful. Too beautiful a morning to stay in bed. Got dressed and yanked YSC out of her bed and we went off round the lake – it was heaven – the lake had those wonderful morning lights reflected in it – the sky was streaked with colour. As we passed the Suisse, General Wheeler and Co. whipped past in their car and cheered us on. Duty all afternoon – very boring . . .

August 10th
Early duty. Quite busy in spots. Hal has invented a ridiculous gadget on his phone so that we know when it's S.O. in C's phone ringing. He loves playing S.O in C. while Micky is away. He is a dear but quite potty. Had letter from Brucie, hoping to arrive 16/17 – what a lovely thought. Had two social rounds to do otherwise all quiet, the place still seems dead. General Lamplough bounced in to see about his fate, to get details and make arrangements. Maggie just back from Colombo – had been entertaining the Captain of the Q.E – and I was told detailed accounts of her visit. Duty again at midnight.

[1] LOKAN's: this was the prefix plus a no. given to signals between London and Kandy – and KANLO for signals between Kandy and London – for this trip only.

August 11th –16th

The days have gone by. And all very busy – signals flying between London and Kandy, and some days didn't know whether I was standing on my head or my heels, and as everyone seemed to fall by the wayside with the dreaded dengue we just had to plod on. I dreaded night duty and almost wept at the thought of going on, and found it hard to concentrate. HH promised she'd take me out of watches just as soon as she could afford to let me – so I hung on to that marvellous thought. The place is very empty without all my playmates and I long to see them all back again bouncing in and out – everything being 'it's the bottom' or 'must go and amuse General so and so for a few minutes' – or 'busy back soon' – dodging SAC – and our wonderful parties at KP, and all of us creeping down the back stairs trying not to disturb the inmates! Sue Pearce got married on 12 th and is now Mrs Philip Richardson, she is away for 5 weeks.

August 17th – 23rd

Brucie arrived today – I got a lift down to the station, just as well as it was raining. Had a lovely breakfast of bacon and eggs on the train, then slept most of the way down. Arrived in Colombo – God it was hot. Clem met me in a large staff Plymouth – we drove round Colombo and saw parts I'd never seen – then on to Ratmalana. After lunch went down to the aero-drome and got news of arrivals from control, then wandered around the field inspecting bombers. Drove to Mount Lavinia for tea – we sat right on the edge of the terrace overlooking the sea: a heavenly wind was blowing spray into our faces. Back to the mess, heard *Hapgift* overhead and tore to the field. A.V.M. Whitworth Jones there but no Bruce – back to mess for a drink – back to the field as we heard the daily plane coming in, and arrived as it taxied up. Brucie jumped out – he looked so pale but how wonderful to see him. We were taken back to the mess for a drink and then driven back to Colombo to catch the 'Kandy Special'. The sun set just as we left and a pink glow spread over everything, sparkled in the water and filtered through the trees. As it got darker there was nothing to be seen except the glow of the fires from the natives' huts, and of course the fireflies. We had supper on the train – got in about 9.30. I had to go on night duty, so had to leave Brucie to the tender mercies of my chums. The next three days, when I wasn't working, we did nothing but walk and talk and see all our friends – and they were all so happy to see him. As we were all working overtime, Brucie went up to Udapussellawa on 21st to stay with his cousin Daphne Cathcart, who lives on a tea plantation in the hills. I didn't ask for leave as I had just had some, but Heather sent me off – and gave me five days to be with him. She also told me to go and settle my life and if I wanted to marry Bruce, she and Micky would do everything they could to help me. The Wren officer in charge of Rear HQ signal office in Delhi was leaving the Wrens, as she as having a baby and wanted to be with her husband – and I could be sent to replace her – I was completely staggered.

August 23rd
Return of the Prodigals, and how wonderful to see them all back – and things will start to hum again. They were all full of English news. I could hardly bear the thought that they were in London last Saturday. They said that everyone at home was very cheerful and optimistic. This place has begun to live again, though no SAC yet.

August 24th
Early duty. SAC's ETA came through as I went off for lunch. he comes this evening. Letter from Brucie looking forward to seeing me on 29th – me too. Back on duty at 6.30. SAC has just arrived, we all felt quite different.

August 26th
Night duty last night, and came off this morning more dead than alive. I have tried so hard to get dengue and join the others, but no luck!! ... Wrote Bruce. Note from HH to say I could now have from Tuesday to Saturday instead of Monday to Friday. Phoned Bruce to tell him and spoke for hours – lovely to hear his voice ...

August 28th
Early duty. Got lift with Hal to Peradeniya. Nothing particular to do so I clambered round and snooped and did odd jobs ... Back and packed – boys I'm off.

August 29th –2nd September
Arrived at Nanaya at 5.45 a.m. – dozed most of the way. It was still dark when I arrived but my Bruce was there to meet me at the station. We drove back to Udapussellawa. Dawn broke slowly – a pale light, silhouetting the mountains, grew over the sky, and slowly every imaginable colour swept over the world. The tips of the mountains became golden and vividly clear as the sun rose – and suddenly darkness was swept away and day was here, though the valleys still lay shrouded in mist. We got to the bungalow about

7a.m – a deep valley lay in front, it was heavenly – a large frangipani tree was on the lawn just outside my window. Daphne was sweet and welcoming – I had a hot bath and breakfast and we sat on the lawn all morning just feasting our eyes. Neighbours came for a drink before lunch. Rested in the afternoon and then went for a walk through the plantation. Back after sunset – early bed.

Meant to get up early next day and go for a walk, but that sorted itself out by sleeping until nearly 8.30. Jumped up and dressed. The morning was clear and lovely and I felt so happy. We took the car and motored over to the Cuthbert Estate, Brooklands. Great sweeps of green terraces and in part just like the rolling hills of Scotland. We were shown round the factory, the tea was already sorted and ready to go. Cuthbert talked too much, otherwise I enjoyed it. We then went to their bungalow for a drink. Started home for lunch about 12.30, sang all the way and had a crazy time. After tea we went for a walk, a gold light over the world – this is really a magical island. Bathed and dined.

It was a wonderfully peaceful five days – we did nothing but go for long walks between tea and dinner every evening – sang at the tops of our voices songs from 'Oklahoma' – got lost in the mists and came back to lovely hot baths, a drink and a huge log fire. I was happier than I can possibly say. We both came back on Saturday 2nd – to find no water in Kandy because of drought – was filthy and so brown that everyone made rude remarks about my heredity!! We both went out to the Officer's club had dinner and danced – and I had to go on duty again at midnight. I got back at 8 a.m., woke Brucie and we had breakfast together. Went for a walk round the lake before lunch. We were supposed to be going up to King's Pavilion for tea but we talked so much that it was 6 o'clock before we knew where we were – he was due to go back to Delhi on Tuesday 5th with the Supremo, who was going up to Delhi in *Hapgift* – he was called to the phone, came back to my room – 'What do you think' he said 'the trip has been delayed 24hrs!' We were ecstatic – we had a quiet dinner together – and then again I had to go on duty at midnight. We pottered about the next day until it was time to go to the station.

September 6th
Saw Brucie off on the train and wandered home ... He rang me from Colombo about 10 ... duty midnight. Dozed off about 4am and woke with a start at 5.45 by the phone ringing – it was Brucie just setting off for the plane.

September 18th

Early duty. Got to office at 8.30, busy for a couple of hours. Went over to Irene to ask if she'd get me copies of the KP photos – it will be done – she's an angel ... Official signal arrived today with my posting to Rear HQ Delhi, in charge of the signal office. It will be a great wrench leaving, but the memories are so wonderful – and I have had an incredibly happy time, and such great friendships ... Got home about 8.p.m. – had dinner in a dream, and suddenly all the wonderful things I have done since I came out here came flooding back and I felt stunned. I wish I wasn't so sentimental!

September 23rd

Came off duty at 8a.m this morning – my very last night watch and it is WONDERFUL. I feel quite different. Pottered most of the day, and snoozed a bit after lunch. Up to Snake Villa, where I found ML and AL about to go out – joined them in smart walk round the lake. Back for tea at Snake Villa, Johnny Papps turned up on horseback with Prince Philip of Greece who is staying with LMB. He is very handsome and unaffected, fair haired and has very ready laugh and we had an amusing time chatting away. Eventually they all went to get ready for Janey's party. After dinner we went across to KP to see how the others were getting on. I was with Johnny and Co. when Arthur came bursting in to say that LMB was coming down to congratulate me on my engagement himself – I was a bit taken aback and anyway I was in an awful mess – however he was awfully sweet 'What's this I hear Susan, another engagement in my H.Q.?' I felt very shy and didn't know quite what to say, as my engagement wasn't public property – yet. HH came to see me later and told me that LMB had announced it at the party!

September 28th –October 9th

The Headquarters are thick with C in C's this morning – ADC's office seething with top boys of every description and size *(for talks re the Quebec Conference)*[1] AL & ML collected me to go to the Chinese lunch and as we passed the War Room we could hardly move for cars and ADCs. When we got to Kandy we were all going slowly in a queue of cars, we went half way round the lake and waited until we saw Carton de Wiart's car come over the bridge and we whisked in after it. WHAT a lunch. I thought it would never end. I was very clumsy with my chopsticks and

[1] Quebec Conference – Future plans for Europe after the war

succeeded in knocking my rice wine over A.L's plate – thank God as it was 100% proof. We all staggered back to work and I nearly fell asleep on my desk. Donald Eckforth came in to see about something and I was saved from passing out altogether. I went home early and repacked my trunk – all the lights failed and I worked by candlelight for the rest of the evening. Donald Erskine Crumb *(who replaced Hank Hanbury as Air ADC to LMB)* has arranged that my luggage goes up to Delhi in *Hapgift.*, and thereby hangs a tale. I had everything organised, my three trunks were going to be met at Colombo, taken out to Ratmalana and shipped on to *Hapgift*. I wrote to warn Brucie as he was going have them collected at Willingdon airport and delivered to Jaipur House, which was now the Wren officers mess. I saw them on to the train at Kandy and never gave them another thought. About five days later *Hapgift* returned from Delhi. Donald E.C. was talking to the captain of the aircraft on the phone and quite casually asked it if my luggage had been delivered, but it had never been seen! – Panic stations – Poor old Donald felt awful – so did I! – Everything I possessed was in my trunks. Arthur gaily said I could have anything out of Maggie's vast wardrobe if the worst happened!. Phone calls were going right left and centre – in fact the police in Colombo were almost brought in. Then I thought of ringing up the Transport Officer in Colombo. The Kandy Special I was told was there and just on the point of coming up. I asked him if would have a look and see if my cases were on the train. Believe it or not they were still in the luggage van, and had been travelling down and up from Kandy for 5 days. There was general post. Donald E.C. said if they would get them off the train before it left, he'd see they were collected and put on *Hapgift* which was going up the next day. I was allowed to send a signal the next day as follows :

FROM: S.A.C.S.E.A.   030541 Z OCT
TO: REAR S.A.C.S.E.A.

RESTRICTED   KAN 1568
                For MASON
Please pass the following to FORTUNE VICEROY'S HOUSE
From MACKIE:
Luggage awaiting collection WILLINGDON AIRPORT ex HAPGIFT
                  T.O.O. 030541 Z OCT
                      (D.S.O.)

Copy to D.S.O. only

and all was accomplished! What it is to be in the right place.

October 8th

My last day in the office – A year ago today I was in London waiting to go, with that awful feeling in my heart of leaving everyone that was dear to me, and going to something unknown --but there has not been a dull moment since! – in spite of the moments of depression, which are inevitable wherever one is. I feel sad at leaving my friends and the wonderful and exciting times we have had, and the stupid things we have done. So much has happened that sometimes I can scarcely believe it.

I went over to say goodbye to General Wedemeyer and General Wheeler. Wedemeyer touched me more than I can say by saying 'You're a grand girl Susan, you've made many friends here – Goodbye, good luck and I'll come up for the wedding. 'I didn't know quite how to answer – I just fled. A little later one of his aides came round to the office with a large envelope – and there was a signed photograph of himself, a large map of South East Asia behind him, typically American, but I thought quite the loveliest gesture. (He came through Delhi in October on his way to replace Stilwell in China. He went to see the Viceroy, Hugh Euston greeted him when he arrived at VH, and he asked 'Are you Bruce Fortune?' – whereupon Brucie stepped forward and said 'No, I am!!' I remember in Kandy after the Supremo's effort at broadcasting the fact that I was engaged, Wedemeyer tackled me on the subject. I told him that it was not yet public – he said in his wonderful drawl 'I promise you I won't tell more than a dozen people'.)

Extract from letter to my mother

'I left Ceylon on 9th October. A car came to collect me at 6.30 as dawn was breaking – I shan't enlarge on that again! – though it has to be seen to be believed. I travelled up in *Sister Anne* – I have told you of the luxury of that! I got more and more excited. We were told that we were going to land an hour earlier than scheduled, and we did. Brucie arrived very soon – he was phoning to find out what our ETA was, to be told plane was just landing! I can't believe that I am back. We went straight to Jaipur House, which now houses both Officers and ratings as there so few of us. This, if I haven't told you before, was Jai's winter palace. It is reasonably small compared with the other Maharajas' palaces in Delhi. Large airy rooms and a lovely swimming pool, though it is usually rather murky. I have a lovely large room on the ground floor with french windows and a huge bathroom, albeit with a tin bath – plenty of hot running water and proper loo. The bath is set in a sunken area with drain in the middle and the bath water is emptied into this where it gurgles away – all very simple! There was a mass of flowers awaiting me in my room – from Gen. Stratemeyer, sweet of him – he is old enough to be my father, but the thought was nice! I have my own telephone in case I have calls when off duty – makes me feel very important! There is another bed in my room, but I hope I shall never have to share. I made a great thing about how boring it would be for a stable companion if I had urgent calls during the night, and how disturbing and all that! However, just to show willing, I suggested that they could use the bed for bods passing through!!"

I settled into my new job, which was not very taxing except when SAC came up and things buzzed. We did not have any night duty, but hours varied according to the amount of work coming in. I had a couple of Wren Officers and three Wren typists and we were kept busy. We had some interesting people about. One was Peter Fleming who ran 'D' (deception) Division *(he was Ian Fleming's brother)*. He was madly deceiving the Japs, us, and I think sometimes himself! We used to try and work out what was true and what was false in the cryptic telegrams he sent back home on what was going on. We pretended that we had succeeded, but of course we had not – it kept us amused. Joan Spens gave me a dear little dachshund puppy whom we named Jeannie – it was delivered to Bruce while I was still in Ceylon, and so Bruce continued to keep her as I could not have her in the mess and besides it was more fun for her to be with all the other dogs at VH, though I had her when I was staying with the Spens' when Bruce was on tour. She would come with me on my rounds at GHQ, and was a wonderful companion. Unfortunately she did not always understand the difference between inside and outside as all the passages at VH were marble. However dear Lady Spens was very sweet about her misdemeanours!

Late one evening when I arrived back in the mess I found a body in the other bed Oh Lord, I thought, another 'guest'. Next morning when the 'body' introduced herself, she was Christine Guthrie and had come to run the aerial photographic section. She shared my room for a couple of weeks and we got on extremely well. We had the same sense of humour and had much in common. I thought that as I might well be forced to have a stable companion that I would rather choose my own, so magnanimously I suggested she stayed put! She eventually became my bridesmaid and is a friend to this day.

During the hot weather kus kus tatting, a sort of grass matting, was hung on the outside of the windows and bheestis *(water carriers)* would come round with a pigskin filled with water and throw it over the tatting, which cooled the hot air coming in. We would take the mattress off our beds and lie on the webbing, which was much cooler. We also put a fan on a chair and hung a wet towel in front of it, so cool air was blown towards us. As Jaipur was a winter palace, there was no form of air-conditioning.

There were many visits from various people from Kandy and it was always good to see them. When SAC came up he would bring Ronnie Brockman, Heather and or Micky, an ADC and perhaps a few others. Little Hal was always a very welcome face, and Brucie and I enjoyed entertaining them.'

Back to Delhi

Bruce and I could communicate when he was on tour. He would send his letters in the Viceroy's daily air bag and they would be delivered to me at my office in Rear HQ. I would have mine sent up to the mail office at V.H. to be put in the daily bag sent to the Viceroy.

Bruce was on tour with H.E. 7th – 16th December to Bombay, Hyderabad and Imphal. I got my first note which he wrote just as he left, and it was waiting for me in the office.

Viceroy's House
New Delhi December 7th
'... Just off, very cold, dark, and rather dreary ...'

Rear Headquarters, New Delhi
December 7th.
'... How comforting to get your letter ... Roundly ticked off by an officious Wren Officer whom I'd never heard of and who is here for three days. She is in the exalted position of being secretary to Admiral Holland – bless her heart. You may laugh!

Christine gave me a letter, and asked me if I could get it over to a certain room in H Block. Being an obliging sort of person said I would put it in the hands of one of my D/R.'s. Some time later the phone rang and I was asked for in person. Announcing that it was none other speaking the voice said 'Oh Mackie this is Second officer (... ??) speaking, secretary to RNIO, *(Royal Naval Intelligence Officer)* what do you want me to do with this letter – it's marked secret and personal, and unsealed?' – while the latter part of this burble was going on I put my hand over the phone and dared her address me in that tone of voice! I told her that she'd better send it back, that I'd only sent it to oblige Christine, and presumably she'd given me the wrong room number. Again she insisted 'What do you want me to do with it?' I said I didn't care and if the D/R was still there to send it back to me. Whereupon she pulled herself to her full height – or from the sound of her voice she did! –'And when you're speaking to your superior officer kindly be more polite' I was so flabbergasted I couldn't speak – I waited in silence until she had put the receiver down and thought, is that the way she uses her two stripes? I know it's silly, but I loathe women in the Services using authority in this way. Perhaps she heard my aside – which was a pity – still, on finding out later who she was and that she was comparatively young and tried to exert her rank to all in this undignified way, it didn't worry me too much. A long story about nothing and very childish – I have been cursing Mrs Pankhurst ever since . . .'

Government House Bombay
December 7th
'. . . Here we are miles away already. Very hot and sticky. We had a very good flight – very cold as you predicted. I slept for about two hours and then drank gimlets with H.E. and Hugh. This is a wonderful place, all bungalows and rambling paths, situated on Malabar Point and surrounded on all sides with water. How I wish you were here . . . We go to Hyderabad tomorrow where life has pantomime prospects' (*We spent 10 days of our honeymoon with the Colvilles at Government House Bombay. We were given Point Bungalow which was at the point of the peninsular, a fantastic position. The whole of the Government House Complex was demolished after partition – rather sad*)

Rear Headquarters, New Delhi
December 8th
. . . 'I have been very busy this afternoon picking up the telephone and hearing jabberings from Indians – most annoying, but quite funny. I can dial the same number six times and get a different number every time – nothing works here. I sat on a chair the other day and it all but gave way under me. I asked a bearer to take it away – he did, and put it at another table, presumably to have the enjoyment of seeing someone finding themselves on the floor! – or plain stupidity – I didn't stop him! I thought it would be rather funny too. Needless to say nothing happened . . . Longing for the 16th' . . .

Falalnuma Castle
Hyderabad, Deccan
December 11th
' Got your wonderful letters last night – what joy they brought me. I too am tearing off those calendar dates – and they seem to go all too slowly. We

are having much too busy a time for my liking and everyone is very tired in spite of the fact that we are only halfway through. Already two banquets are behind us. – (had to stop writing and continue with the unending rounds) . . . I have seen many extraordinary things, many of which I certainly had no idea still went on in the world of today. This place is feudal beyond belief and the ruler a wicked old despot. He has only one legitimate child and hundreds of illegitimates, who throng the dreary interior of his dowdy palace. Hugh, Douglas (Currie) and I have practically had it. The staffs of the various princes etc are so inefficient around here – that we are working 18 hrs a day to try and turn the chaos into demi-chaos.'

Government House
Calcutta
December 13th
'Here we are at yet another destination – and one step nearer home . . . Our flight this morning was a good one and we all spent much of it with eyes tightly closed, attempting to shed the inevitable Hyderabad hangover.

We were all glad to leave the territory of that terrible Nizam. Yesterday evening we all had dinner with him in his private Palace, and it could never have been more spooky. Wretched depressed and haggard women lurked everywhere, and one was brought for special exhibition. She sat on a sofa and shivered and shrank with fear – that such feudalism should be in operation today made me feel rather sick – In absolute contrast to these wretches, whom he called his daughters, were the two Princesses, *(Princess Niloufer and The Princess of Berar)* who were noble of bearing and 'wondrous fair'. They are of Turkish origin and quite European to look at and wear the most beautiful saris . . .'

Wavell of course saw a slightly different side, his way was naturally eased while the ADC's had to deal with the Nizam's inefficient staff. However the dinner party rather shows the meanness of one of the richest men in the world at that time.

Extract from Wavell's Diary
'We spent December 8-13 in Hyderabad. It was very strenuous, but in some ways easier than I expected. The Nizam, of whose eccentricity and personal habits I had heard so much, was in some ways an agreeable surprise. We had a long drive together from the airfield to the Falaknuma Palace where we were quartered. This pretty well exhausted my small talk, for H.E.H *(His Exalted Highness)* was not helpful. Then we paid one

another State Visits and this involved sitting side by side, and making formal conversation for 10 or 15 minutes. We managed quite fairly well, but I had to do practically all the conversation, and it does not come easy to me … There were some rather comic incidents. One was H.E.H. and the champagne. Before the visit the Nizam had written to the Resident expatiating on the high price of champagne and enquiring whether I expected it to be served to me. I told the Resident to relieve H.E.H's mind by telling him that I thought champagne was out of place in war time. However, on this last night the major-domo came to me shortly after dinner began and said the Nizam wished me to drink champagne with him. A champagne glass was placed before me, but no champagne followed and I heard agitated colloquies of the servants with H.E.H. on my left. It turned out that the first bottle opened was flat or corked, and it took some courage to suggest to the Nizam that a second bottle should be broached. This too proved to be flat and there was consternation. Finally someone was found hardy enough to suggest the opening of a third bottle and the Nizam regretfully agreed. But that too was wrong and the champagne was given up. The Nizam explaining to Her Ex and myself the high price the champagne had cost him and the sorrowful waste of money. (The major-domo, a European, explained to me later the H.E.H had bought the champagne years ago and had kept it standing upright with fatal results)'

On the 15th Dec they flew to Imphal, where on the parade ground, which was in a hollow surrounded by hills, on the edge of the Imphal Plain, the Viceroy knighted Generals Slim[1], Christison[2] Scoones[3] and Stopford.[4] Bruce and Hugh Euston both assisted and I have a wonderful photograph of the ceremony.

On 14th January 1945 Brucie accompanied the Viceroy on a trip to Nepal.

Viceroy's House New Delhi
14th January 1945
'Just off at crack of dawn … box for Jeannie arriving about 1600 hrs, with sweeper and all … will think of you all the trip …

[1] Slim: Lieut. General Sir William Slim G.O.C. 14th Army
[2] Christison: Lieut. General Sir Philip Christison C.-in-C. Land Forces S.E.A.C
[3] Scoones: Lieut. General Sir Geoffrey Scoones Commander 4 corps
[4] Stopford: Lieut. General Sir Montague Stopford G.O.C. Burma Command – His telegram to his wife read 'Have been trying to make a lady of you for 22 years. Have today succeeded'

'... the unimaginable joy that I felt when I received your letter on return from the jungle yesterday ... how I wish you were here. It is such a lovely place – and the air is so crisp and clear that my cold has almost vanished. The shooting is rather overdone, I am afraid. We have already bagged 10 tigers and 5 rhinos, and my sporting instinct is rather shattered by the whole proceedings. Here they ring the tiger (or rhino) with elephants, and stretch round a white ring of cloth over which it can't jump. Then with three to four tuskers they proceed to beat it out of cover. When it breaks cover, no matter how bad a shot you are, you have ample opportunity to riddle it with bullets. H.E. and I, however, had quite fun yesterday when in a rhino ring. There were three rhino which alternately charged us, and one felt there was an element of danger and that one was shooting in self defence. Our first shots proved very ineffective and rather bloody, and a very angry rhino was galloping madly about. They are encased in armour plating and their only vulnerable part is a small patch in the neck. One dropped dead. The second after countless hits and near misses dropped dead also. The third went charging round the ring. Eventually, after elephants had stampeded, trumpeting madly in their fright, and maharajas had taken refuge behind trees in terror, the rhino came to its happy hunting ground in a muddy pool.

The only other bit of excitement, was on the day before, when Peter (Coates) shot a tiger in the leg, The tiger resenting this, leaped out of the ring and made off. However the situation was rescued by prompt action of the elephant tribe who fanned out to right and left and made another ring round where they thought the tiger would be. As luck would have it the tiger was there. It resented its encirclement and promptly charged Peter on his elephant and caught the elephant in the hind quarters, causing the beast to stampede. The presence of mind of a certain Nepalese general, who was with Peter, however, saved the situation, and leaning over the back, and using his rifle as a pistol he shot the tiger dead in it's tracks. Thank the Lord we have these little bits of excitement, otherwise 'sport' would not be the word to describe the proceedings. Although I must say that the elephants en masse make a wonderful sight – and the jungle is full of interest.

In addition to shikar, we are amused by the huge brass band which plays, very well I must say, in the camp every evening during dinner and afterwards. After breakfast we have 3 pipers who play rather drearily up and down the camp. At present they are playing a variation of Cock o'the

North', which sounds as though the 'cock' is about to have an egg any moment ... This I hope will get you tomorrow morning, as an aircraft is due any minute now. We have rather a bumpy landing strip in the jungle here, otherwise we are out of touch with the world, save for a L.R. W/T *(long range wireless/ telegraph)* to Delhi ...'

Extract from Wavell's diary
January 19th
'Got back this evening from five days camp in Nepal Terai with Maharaja. The party shot twelve tigers and six rhino. It was good fun and a very pleasant change in an attractive part of the country.

We were very comfortable and the atmosphere was very friendly. The old Maharaja (Joodha) was very well and in good form, I liked him. There was a ceremony (spring festival) on the morning of the 18th, at which H.H. and his family wore their gorgeous head-dresses, solid with diamonds, pearls, emeralds and rubies and topped with birds of paradise; and H.H and suite came in after dinner on the last evening to make a short speech and propose my health to which I replied and proposed the Maharaja's: otherwise there was no social contacts and we lived in separate camps'...

However, Bruce did say to me later that at one point H.E. handed him his rifle saying 'I've had enough'

Visit to Jaipur

February 1945
Extracts from a letter to my mother
'We got back from Jaipur the day before yesterday. It was the most wonderfully happy seven days. Though I started my leave unofficially at noon last Wednesday 7th, we did not leave until 9th. Bruce rang up at 2 o'clock – after being cut off three times – something we get very used to – to say he'd collect me at 2.30. I had everything packed, and from then on I was FREE – too good and wonderful to be true. Brucie arrived and we set off to do some shopping to buy the odd necessity – like a tooth brush! – then back to the House for tea. The place was so quiet – H.E. was off on tour to Mysore, and of course, the other ADC's were with him. It was strange not to have the usual hubbub in the ADC room. Brucie decided that he must have some exercise so dashed off and had a strenuous game of tennis with

a lovely Indian, known as J.C. – because of his bearing and beard! – and who was always available to play, coach, or just throw balls to people like myself who needed endless practice. I watched for a little and then went back to the House to have a bath. We shot off later to have drinks with the Curries and walked back just after 9 o'clock. We changed very rapidly while Rhamet went ahead to the train with our suitcases and bedding rolls to get our berths ready for us. To our surprise and horror we found the station master waiting for us at the entrance plus a Viceregal servant all dolled up in his scarlet and gold. We were escorted to our carriage and found, as usual, everything ready.

I slept the whole way and we arrived at Jaipur about 5.30a.m. where we were met by one of Jai's ADC's. We were driven off to the guest house and given some tea. David Clowes, one of the Governor of Bengal's ADC's, had arrived ahead of us and we went to have a word with him. After drinking gallons of tea I retired to have a sleep. I was wakened at 9 o'clock and got up – very slowly – trying to believe that I was really on leave and miles away from Delhi. Bruce came to collect me and we had a huge breakfast. Just as we were finished David appeared, having been out riding, and joined us. After breakfast the three of us were driven into Jaipur – a wonderful unspoilt Indian town – no large shops only the ones open onto the streets, with owners sitting outside on their hunkers, watching the world go by or inviting one in to have a look. It was all so very colourful and picturesque. We went to the museum to collect the curator who was to accompany us – a grand old man dressed in a fitted black coat and baggy white trousers, which tapered at the ankles. The museum, approached by a wide flight of steps was huge and ornate with filigreed pink sandstone – the porch was painted with frescoes of all the past maharajahs, in their fabulous bejewelled headresses and gaudy finery.

The city is surrounded by a wall nearly 300 years old with various ornately carved gateways – it was absolutely fascinating. The Pink Palace is in the centre of the town and houses Jai's senior wife – Jai is so European I found this strange, but I suppose like Buchan it was arranged when he was very young and it has to be. Ayesha his chosen wife, whose father is the Maharajah of Baroda, is simply gorgeous, and is always with him and not in purdah as the one in the Pink Palace who incidentally, has produced the next Maharajah.

We stopped to see some of the brass engravers – a little man was sitting cross legged working away, and further on a small boy was doing intricate work with his head bowed so close to his work – I thought how awful, the work he was doing was so fine that he probably would be blind before he was twenty. Next we visited a carpet industry. We drove up a narrow street, got stuck and had to get out and walk – we were greeted by the most ghastly smell. The drainage from the nearby houses – only too near – was running down the gutters. David asked – not so tactfully – what was happening to improve Jaipur drainage. I couldn't laugh, I was too busy holding my breath! We came to an archway with WELCOME written in large letters. Inside was a courtyard – on one side, under cover, were five large looms with a row of small boys seated on a bench in front of them. The major-domo stood nearby, chanting. It was explained to us that the note he was chanting denoted the colour to be used. It was intriguing to watch these small boys with such nimble fingers doing such work – but sad all the same to see their young lives being used thus. Nearby were men crawling about clipping the finished carpets.

Next day we went to Ramgarh about twenty miles out of Jaipur. Jaipur is in a valley surrounded by low bare hills. Lots of stunted growths and feathery trees. The plains are sandy and covered with cactus and thick with wild game – if you are lucky a tiger might cross your path!

Ramgarh is a paradise overlooking an enormous lake with hundreds of deep creeks and backed by hills. The shores are steep and have a fringe of coarse grass, then a thick jungle of tall pampas grass. At one end Jai has built what he calls a weekend bungalow. It is huge and the inside is like a modern London store show room! It had been opened up for us and so we prowled round. The décor was too lush for words. The large entrance hall had a gaming table and cocktail bar. The library was surrounded by bookcases with fancy metal work on the doors. However on closer inspection we found that the books were false – ornate leather book backs had been bought by the yard! The kitchens were lined with frigidaires. Bruce and I went upstairs to inspect the bedrooms – their bedroom had an enormous bed raised on a shallow dais. and one sank into a cloud of comfort. Ayesha's dressing room was surrounded by cupboards with pink tinted mirrored doors – very flattering!

Garden furniture had been put out on the lawn, and we sat overlooking the lake. On the terrace below was a swimming pool and from there a broad flight of steps led down to the lake, where a motor boat, painted royal blue and white with blue and white upholstery on the seats and named – surprise surprise – Bluebird, awaited us. We set off sinking into the luxurious cushioned chairs. My eyes were, as they continued to do the whole week, popping out of my head with amazement.

Crocodiles were abundant and lying all over the banks. We tried to stalk them by shutting off the engines and gliding up one of the creeks, but they sensed us very quickly and just slipped quietly into the water. Unfortunately we had only brought shotguns with us, which weren't much good against their thick skins – but how I longed for one – all those lovely bags and shoes! Eventually, just for fun we tried stalking from the land – it was exciting to see how close we could get, and to see them so close up, lying there sunning themselves but never far from the water. The birds round and about gave their alarm very noisily and the crocs all slid into the water and disappeared.

Bruce suddenly saw geese on the far side of the lake, so we called for the boat and set off in chase. As we drew nearer the other side there was a flurry in the water and a great flock of geese rose into the air and flew over us. Bruce took a shot at them, and missed – he thought. Determined as he is – he was not going to give up. He and one of the shikars went ashore, and David and I set off in the boat to try and beat them up towards them. We were quite far out when David shouted 'What's that?' – and there floating in the water was Brucie's goose. We brought it in and went on. Sadly the man at the wheel spoilt our tactics by shutting the engine off too late, frightening the geese who then flew in the wrong direction. An hour later we picked Bruce up – he'd had no success and was thrilled when we showed him the bird we'd landed.

It was getting quite dark and the geese were wheeling over us, it was a magnificent sight. They circled over us with an incredible whirring of wings, then gradually fanned out into a long line, merged together again as they circled back over us, getting higher and higher, and eventually disappearing over the hill.

We came home as the sun was disappearing, leaving a warm glow over the world. The drab colour of the hills was transformed with every light and shade of the evening. The water was streaked with the colours of the dying sun. We got home about 8 o'clock and entered the gates of the city. Its two towers were lit with pink lights. All the city was awake – the shops were lit with candles or oil lamps and some with electricity. The shopkeepers squatted, wrapped in blankets, chatting away noisily to each other. As there are few lights in the streets themselves there is a lovely glow from the shops. It is a fascinating sight rather like an illustration from a fairy tale book. We arrived home very tired and after a welcome drink, drifted off to have baths, and after dinner we had an early night. I had been persuaded to go riding next morning, and the next thing I knew was a cup of tea being put under my nose at 7.30. It was glorious out, the ground was flat with low scrub and we had an exhilarating canter.

Next evening we went to watch for tiger. In the jungle behind the house there was a tower and below, in a hollow, was a circle of stone in which a wretched goat was tied up – this was the tiger trap. When the tiger leaps on its kill the place becomes ablaze with light and the poor tiger has had it. We sat up in the tower and waited for a long time but apart from some grumblings in the jungle, nothing happened and we retired to bed.

The shikar came the next morning and said that a tiger turned up shortly after we had left – but we didn't believe him!

Another day we were collected by the shikar in an open shooting brake and went off into the wild. A few black buck crossed our path and we chased after them. It was most exciting as we wove through the rough scrub, hanging on like grim death – at least I was! – The black buck won. I found these huge open spaces really quite awe inspiring – nothing, but nothing in sight as far as the eye could see – waving grasses and spiky out-crops of cactus and scrub, and the all enveloping sky – and us – incredible.

We were invited up to the Palace for lunch with Jai and Ayesha, which was quite an experience. It was rather like an Arabian Night scene. Lots of marble and pillars and fabulous formal gardens. Ayesha – who is tall and slender with gorgeous dark shoulder length hair, was wearing the most beautiful sari, looked fantastic – was so sweet, and of course Jai too is absolutely charming. We had a delicious lunch, very European and all very informal.

That evening we were invited to dinner by the Prime Minister of Jaipur. I was surprised how very at home we felt. Their son spoke the most per-fect English with absolutely no accent whatsoever. I asked him if he had been at school in England, but he had not. It was a lovely evening and everyone was so charming. It was the first time that I had really come in contact with an Indian family – and I was thrilled'

March 3rd
Brucie had told me that a seat had been reserved for me in their enclosure for the V.C. Parade. A car was sent to take me to the Red Fort where the parade was to be held. It was a most moving ceremony. I was really rather overwhelmed. Needless to say the V.C.'s were mostly posthumous. The lit-tle ghurka wives, with lots of silver on arms and ankles and with their faces completely hidden, were led up to the Viceroy to receive their husband's

medal. I doubt very much if they knew what was happening. It was really very sad. Lots of martial music and lots of people – but all so very sad.

Visit to Agra

At last the long awaited trip to Agra. Brucie collected me about 6.p.m. and we left driven by our faithful smiling Nana. It was getting dark and so we saw little of the countryside as we drove south – and apart from a few lumbering bullock carts with drivers who were, as usual, fast asleep, we saw little traffic – but the bullocks kept plodding on.

It was quite dark when we got to Agra – the sky was clear and the stars very bright, and the moon was coming up. We went straight to the Taj and walked into those magical gardens – pools, which stretched their length, made long shafts of light. The gardens were full of shadows, and at the far end, the mausoleum seemed translucent against the blue black sky, and the stars, like fireflies, surrounding it. We walked up to the forecourt and were let in by an attendant chowkidar. We took off our shoes and the warm marble was like velvet beneath our feet. Inside was eerie, full of emptiness and soundlessness. There was no light as such, but light was emanating from the glowing white marble walls. We were the only people there and everything was so quiet – we talked in whispers.

Coming out we walked down and sat on a marble seat facing the mausoleum. The moonlight now engulfed everything. The pools were silver slashes and the building was glowing as if lit from inside – it was quite miraculous. By now I was so tired that I was having difficulty in focusing – but that made it seem even more unreal.

We arrived home just in time for me to get to the office. It all seemed like a dream. Had I really been there, I ask myself?

March 20th
The Viceroy left for the U.K this afternoon for talks with the P.M. and Sir John Colville (Governor of Bombay) arrived about midday to take over as Acting Viceroy in Wavell's absence.

Extracts from letters to my mother
April 26th

... 'The new Wavell Theatre was opened and the Colville's took a large party to the opening night. We had dinner first on the terrace looking on to the Mughal gardens – it was wonderful and a heavenly night, deep, deep blue sky and bright stars, and the terrace was softly lit. The theatre was open to the skies – just as well – as the night was so warm. Edith Evans and Dorothy Hyson were the star performers. They had been playing for the troops in the front for some weeks with the result they shouted a bit – still it was most enjoyable. I have a press photo, which was taken during the show, their Ex's are in the middle and Bruce and I appear behind them in the corner. Some people are roaring with laughter, but Brucie and I and the rest in our row look very engrossed and serious – we look awful! Afterwards we all went back to the House where a supper party had been arranged. Small tables had been laid on the terrace and the trees were strung with lights. The cast arrived eventually – Dorothy Hyson who looked lovely on the stage, but I thought was awful close up – and we all sat down to supper. They had someone playing the piano – it was very romantic. Their Ex's seemed to enjoy it as well. We danced until nearly 3 a.m. – I loved it. Brucie and I had a lovely old-fashioned waltz together, which went for ages – heaven.'

May 1st

... 'Had a wonderful day last Sunday. I took the whole day off. Brucie came to collect me at 7.30 and with lovely smiling Nana driving us, we took off for a day's shooting, taking Jeannie with us. There was a fairly cool breeze blowing, which helped as the temperature was rising very quickly. We went about 20 miles before we had breakfast. I changed into drill trousers and a bush shirt that Brucie had brought for me. After our picnic breakfast we went off again, keeping our eyes open for black buck. I heard some wild peahens – so we decided to get one of these. We chased one for ages – I walked at one side of the scrub and tried to beat it towards Brucie. Eventually we doubled back and saw one fly up into a tree just above the car. The growth around was very thick and full of acacia thorns. I stayed where I was to distract it, while Brucie got closer to it. I was busy picking thorns out of my hand, when I heard a flurry of wings and a shot. Climbing back on to the road I found Bruce and Nana trying to get hold of it – it had fallen just out of reach and right among the thorns. Poor little Nana was leaning right over the bushes, which were growing on the side of a deep drop. I hung on to Bruce, who was hanging on to Nana, but all the little fellow could produce was a handful of tail feathers. The bird was wedged in the thorn bushes. We lifted a large stick off a couple of passing Indian boys and levered it out – and off we set again. We turned off the road and through an Indian village – it was getting hotter and hotter, the car was scorching to the touch. Now and then a coolish gust of wind would come – otherwise it was just hot air blowing at us.

Eventually after driving over rough ground we saw some buck and drove the car behind a clump of trees. Brucie set off, complete with his pith helmet! Poor little Jeannie was panting, and the water we had brought for her had got so hot, however she lapped it up. I sat in the car, but it became like an oven, so I hopped out. The ground, though of sand, was hard and crunchy with salt and heat. Nana found a little clump of trees and thorn bushes where it would be cooler for me to sit. So I ensconced myself there and watched Brucie in the distance appearing and disappearing in his efforts to stalk the buck. When he disappeared altogether, I settled down to read the paper, and learned more about the San Francisco Conference[1] than I'll ever know – got tired of that and went on to the German atrocities – and was revolted – so lay back and snoozed. I became so thirsty, but daren't touch the water – there was only one flask of iced lemon and the bottles of beer had become very warm Brucie let me have a tiny drop earlier on, but wouldn't take any himself – and he advised me not to unless I absolutely had to – better to wait until the sun was lower. I had no watch – and he seemed to be away for ages – and I got quite worried, imagining him collapsing with heat and all sorts of awful things. I wandered over to an old well to see if there was any water, so I could perhaps cool the beer down – but the water was far too far down. As I came back four bullock carts, with gay trappings and full of people, passed raising clouds of dry dust. Jeannie suddenly made off in the opposite direction – I looked back and there was Brucie, looking for all the world as if he'd just been fighting in the desert, complete with rifle. The salt was caked hard on his lips and he was filthy – but he'd had a wonderful time! He'd seen his buck and was going back later hoping to get it. I mixed him a shandy with the iced lemon and tepid beer and he drank three glasses straight off! The salt on his lips was awfully difficult to remove – I had to pick it off.

I managed to make him wait until later before setting out again, we then drove to where he had seen the buck, but the whole countryside had sud-

[1] San Francisco Conference: Planning for the foundations of a free, civilised and united world

116

denly become alive with herds of cattle – and no buck! We passed through a village – there was just room enough for the car between the mud huts and we could see the people inside – asleep – with their cattle and domestic animals wandering in and out. Two tiny naked boys were washing at the village well, and took to their heels when they saw us! We had to go over rough ground again where we saw a party of small boys, who pointed out to us where the buck had gone – we followed their direction – but no sign. I was jolly thankful because if he'd gone off again there was only one bottle of liquid left for him, and very warm at that. You have no conception of the thirst that overcomes you.

We set off home and got back tired and exhausted about 6.30, collecting my evening things from Jaipur on the way, and went straight up to the House. It was heaven to tumble into a bath and get changed. When I was ready I found a cool drink waiting for me. Brucie came in followed by t'other Bruce *(Bruce Omerod, one of The Auk's ADC's and known as t'other Bruce)* close on his heels, to ask how tired I was. I knew they had something up their sleeves, which they had! So we all, including Suzanne, *(Suzanne Marshall and later one of my bridesmaids)* went out to dine together. We were all in cracking form and sang at the tops of our voices all the way out to Old Delhi. We had a hilarious evening and later went back to the C in C's house. T'other Bruce tried to make us all go into the pool for a swim after mid-night. But by then we were all too tired. A heavenly moonlight night and the drive back to Jaipur House was beautiful – but Lord I was tired'

May 8th VE Day
'It is difficult to believe it is all over, how wonderful it is for all of you at home – how I wish I were there. This last fortnight has seemed like a bit out of a thriller. We heard the armistice was signed unofficially about 9 o'clock,

I have a phone by my bedside and had rang up GHQ to tell them to ring me directly the news came through – we wouldn't believe it until we heard it from the War Office, which we did eventually this morning. After the false alarm last week it came as a sort of anti climax.' *(Hitler had been reported dead and Germans had surrendered in Italy)*

Bruce had to go with H.E. to Broadcasting House this evening, as he was talking just after the Prime Minister. I listened to it from his room and when they played 'Pomp and Circumstance' I could have howled. The whole thing has been such a ghastly waste of life. The attitude 'why not be glad now it's all over' when so much has happened and so many have paid the price, won't help anybody, but it sobers one up and makes one think. But I do thank God it is over and that Brucie has recovered so much, and do realise, and am thankful, that we are two of the lucky ones. We have heard that Brucie's father has at last come home after five long years as a P.O.W. which is wonderful.[1] After he had a stroke some months ago, the Germans were going to repatriate him – but he refused saying that he came in with the 51st and that he would go out with them. He must be a wonderful man ...'

May 22nd ...
'On May 16th there was a March Past to celebrate V.E, followed in the evening by a State Dinner party. The March Past was held in the cool of the evening. I had to be up at V.H. ready to leave at 5.40. I found Bruce looking so handsome and smart in his kilt and in shirtsleeve order. I went in the first car with Hugh and two others. We arrived at Connaught Circle – which was crammed with people – the car drew up just in front of the saluting dais, and just as I got out a colossal gust of wind practically blew everything off including me and I had to hold my skirt to protect my maidenly modesty! In front of us on the great expanse of grass four lines of soldiers were drawn up, carrying the national flags of all the Allies – it was a wonderful sight. Behind them the Rajputs had a 40 strong pipe band, with bagpipes as well as drums and attached paraphernalia. Two other car loads arrived from the House, and then Her Ex and Mary Colville. A few seconds later a policeman on motorbike roared up followed by the C in C's car -- and there was a General Salute. All the flags were brought up to the salute – it was a fine sight as they fluttered in the wind. Another outrider roared up, and H.E's car drew up. I was very proud of Brucie as he jumped out and opened the car door and stood to attention and saluted H.E. as he got out. The National Anthem was played followed by a Royal Salute. The pipers struck up again and led by Bruce and Hugh doing the slow march, H.E. went round the lines of flag bearing soldiers. When that was over they changed to a quick march and they led H.E. and the C. in C. to the dais. The march past then began. There were a huge number of newsreels and cameras snapping – they dashed out and got themselves into the most extraordinary positions to take the shots – everything but lie flat on the

[1] Brucie's father was Knighted in June 1945 for his tireless work for the welfare of prisoners of war

ground. After gun salutes and National Anthems, nine Spitfires flew low overhead.

Bruce told me that he would not be able to see me after the parade until about 8.30, so after we had all been deposited back at the House, to commandeer a car for myself to get back to Jaipur and ask the driver to collect me again at 8.15. Bruce wanted me to come early so's he could deposit me in the throng before going about his duties with their Ex's – however he was already on duty when I got there! We were all foregathered in the ballroom – Brucie arrived and came and whispered words of encouragement and said he loved my dress – which made me feel wonderful – then he had to dash off again. A table plan and general procedure plan was thrust into my hand. A quick glance showed me that Ruth Merrill and myself were seated at the entrance end of the dining room, which meant that we'd have to follow Her Ex. out at the end of dinner.

At 9.15 we were all lined up. Brucie appeared leading Their Ex's. As they went down the line Bruce presented everyone by name – how he remembered all the 60 names is more than I can think – even though we were shoved into order! We then were all ushered into the State dining room. The long table was awash with silver and crystal. Flowers and lights all the way down the centre, the only other lighting was over the numerous portraits of past Viceroys and at the far end of the dining room in a huge but shallow alcove framed in light, the most wondrous gold plate. It was all most impressive.

Just as I got to my place Brucie, who was just coming back from getting their Ex's seated, leant over and said 'well done darling'! That made me feel very good. There was a khitmatgar behind each chair, lighting was very flattering with the dimness round the room and the softness over the table[1]. A band was playing on the terrace below and after dinner a piper played round the table. After the toast to 'the King Emperor' H.E. made a short speech, then the signal to retire was given – we all rose and our chairs were whipped back by unseen hands – and we stood back. Her Ex. walked down in front of us then at the door turned, curtseyed deeply and left. Then Ruth and I went, turned at the door – and curtseyed – and funnily enough I wasn't a bit nervous though I thought I would be.

Afterwards we all went into the garden – the whole place was lit, pools

[1] A small card with the Wavell unsignia topped with a coronet,was placed in front of each guest with the menu, in French. I can't remember what we had on that evening but I had dinner at the House with Brucie the night before they all went to Simla and I have kept the card.we had – Souffle de Saumon followed by Poulet Roti then Rognons en Brochettes, this would be a typical menu.

and fountains sparkling. The great basins at the corners on top of the house, which were in fact designed as fountains, were lit from below and inside the basin was aglow with red lighting and swirling smoke and searchlights were sweeping the skies. It all looked like a spectacular film setting. In the gardens people were wandering about – the evening dresses and colourful uniforms, the sparkling fountains and the water rippling over the pools – unreal. The pipers played and when they were not the band took over. I got stuck with some people, but Bruce rescued me by coming up and saying my presence was requested elsewhere! We departed and joined Hugh Euston who was sitting with some others telling the most fantastically funny stories. They all had huge glasses of brandy and so had Bruce and they were having a wonderful time... It ended at midnight. It was the most fairytale evening.

I have been asked to stay at the House for a week. Their Ex's have gone up to Simla and have taken everyone except Bruce, Felicity and Archie John. Felicity asked me if I would like to come and spend the week with them all – I didn't know quite what to say, so I consulted Bruce, who told me that she had already asked him if he thought it might be a lovely change for me. A LOVELY CHANGE!! My goodness me!! Bruce picked me up yesterday from the office and we collected my things from Jaipur House. He took me up to my room after lunch and I found everything had been unpacked and in its place – I think that I am becoming very spoilt – I have a wonderful room, and so air conditioned that I had to have a blanket last night I was so cold, and coming out from the room is like walking into an oven.

The walk to the office is only about a couple of hundred yards, not too to far to walk in this hot weather – I am fortunate indeed.'

June 7th
...Wavell returned today from the U.K

Visit to Simla

June 22nd
... Wavell and his entire staff left on the 22nd June for Simla, where the talks were to take place on the future of India. Brucie sent me a note just before he left. Delhi now seems quite lifeless, and I feel a little bereft.

Extracts from letters exchanged while Brucie was in Simla

Rear headquarters, New Delhi
June 22nd .
... 'How wonderful to get your note – I don't feel so lonely. I cannot really believe that you are not just a few hundred yards away – this is the first time for five whole months that we've been parted – so I mustn't 'mope' as you say – and I won't either.

I saw your plane flashing in the sun as she disappeared into the blue ... It does seem so funny writing to you again – the only advantage is that I can talk on without interruption and ruderies, or look up and find you fast asleep! How's our wee Jeannie? Was she a good girl in the plane? I'd love to hear she'd peed all over Charles[1] or something or someone! I shall tell you about the riding tomorrow night. I shall stagger back and be a good 'dooty' officer. Saturday night is always an amusing night – as you run round looking for the girl friend for the boy, and conducting lost escorts wandering apparently unintentionally into bedrooms, and guide them to the sitting room!!

I wandered up with my letter to you myself – as I could find no other to do it. I knew of no short cuts so went up to North court to find my way as directed by you. I found myself in the Council Room, and looked round – very awe-inspiring. Wandered further on – after going on pretty aimlessly for some time I knocked on a door and pushed it open to be greeted by a lavatory seat – that wasn't much help. A little further on a gesticulating Babu directed me towards Harrison's office and the letter was safely delivered.'

Viceregal Lodge, Simla.
June 22nd
'We have arrived safely with no mishaps. A wonderful run up the hill all the cars went like birds and we must have done it in record time. Jeannie behaved very well and slept or looked out of the window all the way. She insisted on sleeping on Charles' lap and the latter needless to say was rather nervous; but all was well and she ate all the ginger biscuits – I drank too many gimlets and too much beer so fell asleep after lunch and woke up to see the heights of Simla towering in view. It is cooler but not so cool as all that. Just as many monkeys and the sewage still precipitates down the

---

[1] Charles Rankin assistant to the Viceroy's Private Secretary

mountainside (beware those who picnic by some lovely stream!)... I do hope that you are going to be able to come for a few days...'

Rear Headquarters, New Delhi
June 23rd
'Just got your lovely letter ... I thought Jeannie would probably choose Charles – he seems fated – still I'm glad she wasn't sick all over him. I should have hated the plane to be mid-air with his flow of language!!

I'm longing to hear of your first view of Ghandi, and all the fireworks and/or pantomime that ensues. I must write to Maudie to thank her for asking me to stay with her. I phoned Robert this afternoon to ask him about it. He says he can't possibly get away – and incidentally for some reason I insisted on calling him Douglas all the time.

I don't think I can get up at the moment – it would mean dashing up tomorrow which I can't do, and with Joanna off to get married on Thursday and Tim goes on leave on Sunday, it just can't be done. I may manage later if things are quiet, but I think on the whole its better to leave it.

There is a terrific dust storm blowing up – I am battening everything down – jolly good sailor I am! Our pool has suddenly become full of lovely clear water, so I expect the pool up at the House will be clear once more. Christine is in a crazy mood, running about like Aphrodite rising from the waves and imitating a Grecian maiden – dancing with a towel. She's mad.

I'm riding tomorrow morning at 6.30. (tell George that I am taking great care of Minnie) Tim is taking me out – so I'll be a physical and mental wreck when I get back – 'keep those knees in' – phew! She's taking me along by the river so's I'll know how to get there on my own when she goes on leave. 'I hope' she said 'you have ordered your horse at 6.30?' – I said that I had, but forgotten to be wakened. 'I'll waken you' she said quickly. When I asked her how, she said 'I'll come down' which seemed reasonable enough – some one's crazy – I fear it is me.

The other evening Christine was standing in our room in the nude, as usual, when she heard movement at the kuss kuss at the french window. Hastily covering herself just in time to greet an RAF m/t driver who walked boldly in –

'This the Air Commodore's 'ouse?'

Christine, drawing herself up and pulling the towel round her more tightly, informed him that it was the Wren Officer's Mess. The poor little fellow went scarlet and with 'Christ almighty' turned and fled...'

... 'The eve of the great conference and rather like the lull before the storm! I have just shaken Ghandi and Jinnah by the hand. The former was rather a pleasant old man and a real sight for the eyes in his dhotie. The crowds that gather round him are endless and Simla's population has gone up by several thousands in the last week.

Jeannie is very well and full of beans. I have put her on a tonic so that when she return to the plains, she will be more capable of standing the rigours of Delhi. She sends you her love and a nice wet lick ... Jeannie has just met her first monkey and made a very dishonourable retreat. So dishonourable was it that one of the monkeys chased her up the path amid screeches and yells of applause from his brothers up the trees! I must go, we are about to enter into a dinner party! ...'

Rear Headquarters, NewDelhi
June 26th

'... I did have to laugh when I read of our Jeannie's escapades – she is truly learning life through her errors. In spite of her retreat she is, you must admit, showing greater courage than we thought she had in her. Went for a wonderful 'blow' on Minnie this evening – it was heaven getting right away, it is the only thing that saves me while you are away ... Christine and I have come to the conclusion that sometimes we 'sit and sweat' other times we just 'sweat' – funny? Yes? No? she is lying at the moment with a towel round her middle and one over her face crying pathetically 'Susan – what is one to do?' I ask you darling, what is one to do? I find that if I lick myself thoroughly I can retrieve quite a lot of the all important salt!! The things we do for England! Christine has just shown her eyes from under her towel to say that someone asked her the other day why she wasn't married 'I always thought', he said, 'you'd be such a good person for Tom'. 'So did he', said Christine feelingly, remembering the drunken old man! She thinks that one day all her sins will come back on her. 'You know things do – for five minutes or so', said Christine going into fits of giggles. She really is a wonderful tonic ... Had a wonderful ride yesterday morning with Tim – it was beautifully cool. I saw her out of the corner of my eye looking me up and down, and I wondered how long we'd go before she said anything. She did eventually suggest that I held my reins 'this way' and 'sat that way' – giving me demonstrations each time. However besides all that it was really heavenly. I felt so well, and sang loudly. It was so lovely going through the trees on the golf course, and then getting out to the open country by the river surrounded by miles and miles of open ground. Everything was so still, and the pink hazy lights of the sun were spreading over everything. We didn't see a soul and I was very happy. When I got back I had a bathe before breakfast and then, I'm ashamed to say, after breakfast I fell fast asleep – and woke up in a pool of sweat and prickly heat on my forehead, which I'm dealing with as rapidly as possible...'

Viceregal Lodge, Simla
June 27th
'Just got another lovely long letter from you. So glad to hear you had a happy ride with Tim, without any ruderies ... The conference goes on. They have just adjourned for a day and a half, having hedged all morning and got nowhere. They are a strange collection of God knows what – senile and crooked – hiding underneath a placid exterior, and treachery which stops at nothing. A few of them straight from jail to the council table of the Viceroy.

Ghandi is not attending the Conference for reasons you will have read about. We rather think it may also be due to a half-hour talk on W.V.S. activities from Her Ex to which the poor little man was subjected!! – That woman...'

Viceregal Lodge, Simla
June 30th
'Just another mid-night scrawl. This time after a very good E.N.S.A. concert of classical music. At the end they sang 'ma Calla Herring' and I very nearly wept. Aren't I a sentimental old sod?... The rains have descended again and visibility is nix. Also the conference has adjourned till 14th July. I laughed at the description of Christine, she really is a scream as well as very good companion ... Her Ex has extended an invitation to you to come up and stay for a long weekend when you can. So if you can, I think it would be a good idea if you could possibly get away for any time at all. She was very sweet about it and said it would be a change from Delhi for you, so do try darling ... Sir Patrick Spens came over yesterday for a talk with H.E. and asked very tenderly after you. He is as rotund as usual and even more Pickwickian!...'

Jaipur House, New Delhi July 1st
'It was comforting to hear your voice this evening, I had just that minute

got back from the office from a truly hectic day . . . It has really been quite fun – though for 15 minutes I thought I'd had it and that I'd, not so gently, be thrown out on my neck! A signal came this afternoon from LMB to old Charlie[1] requesting a reply to a signal we received the day before yesterday. The reply was sent yesterday and I informed them of this – but it had not been received – panic – as this was a highly secret and personal message. I rang GHQ cypher office – they had no trace – more panic! I had to confess all to uncle Charles, who came and sat in my office while I made people jump to it at GHQ. While Lane and I sat drafting out a signal 'Mounbatten from Lane' making up some sort of story, GHQ rang up to say they'd tracked it down, and horrors they'd sent it unciphered on an open line!! I tried to be as calm as possible, and as quiet as possible – it was very difficult – but I just managed it – just. There was nothing we could do except of course to repeat the signal. Uncle Charles was sweet, he even called me Susan! – I could have wept. We both sent poste hastes – he to LMB and me to Charles St Quintin[2] – and hot and sticky we closed the office. By that time I thought it was all really rather funny – got back overflowing with high spirits, though just a bit tired. And then to get your call was so wonderful . . . I hope I will be able to come up next week . . .'

Jaipur House, New Delhi July 3rd
'. . . I feel a completely different person – I have had a bath! and it has done wonders. The kus kus tatting has been removed from doors and windows – and the last light of the evening is spreading itself across the sky – it is all so peaceful and the birds are singing.

I don't feel nearly so far away from you having spoken to you twice today and had such a lovely long letter, and will deal with all your requests. Fizzie seems a bit vague – I am having lunch with Kath Tweed and Peter Fleming tomorrow and she will be there so I'll see what arrangements she has made . . . I have phoned the controller's office and am getting your keys at 2.30 and will get your shirts, trousers and cheque book . . .'

Jaipur House, New Delhi July 4th
. . . 'All is arranged – and we come up on Friday – Fizzie will collect me . . . I can hardly believe it . . .'

---

[1] Major General Sir Charles Lane: the Supremo's Representative in Delhi
[2] Charles St Quintin: Micky Hodges' replacement as Signal Officer in Chief

Visit to Simla

July 1945 Letter to my mother
'Just got back from my five heavenly days in Simla, I wrote to you from the office the day I left – I was so excited that I hardly knew what to do with myself.

A bevy of servants from Viceroy's House came and collected my suitcase and sleeping roll just after eight and after that I chatted with Christine Guthrie – had dinner and a bath – and by that time it was nearly 10p.m. when Felicity Wavell arrived to pick me up. We were met at the station by the station master who led us to this red monster, which was the Viceregal carriage. Our compartment was enormous. There were two beds on which the bearer had already laid our bedding rolls – lovely white sheets, and our nighties tastefully laid on top. An arm chair to relax in, and in the corner a wash basin. There was also an adjoining bathroom – with a bath! It was all too fantastic and I couldn't help poking around to see what else I could find. Felicity's remark 'What, all this grandeur and no air conditioning?' made me laugh.

We arrived at Kalka at 6.30 next morning and had breakfast at the station. It was so wonderfully cool – I felt a different person after the sticky heat of Delhi. I could have shouted with joy and run for miles. We started our drive up at 7.15. It was a wonderful journey. We climbed slowly as the road twisted and turned up the mountain. Soon the valley was miles below us. We got deeper into the hills as the road, with a sheer drop on one side, curved its way upwards. It took us three and half-hours to climb 55 miles. The mountains seemed never ending – their sides literally folded their way down and deep valleys stretched between them. Some of them were thickly wooded with magnificent pines: others were every shade of green and brown. Lower down there were terraces of cultivation. The morning sunshine sent soft shadows and lights over everything. Truly they are the mighty Himalayas. Eventually travelling up the side of the mountain we saw Simla, long before we got there, perched on a ridge and stretching its way across the hillside, but as we curled round and up in a series of S bends we lost sight of it.

At last we arrived at Simla where a car was waiting for us. We hadn't got very far when for some reason I looked down at my hand and saw that one of the diamonds in my ring was missing – panic stations. However, I looked down, and there it was on the rug of the car – what an awful moment – was I not lucky?

We drove through the gates of Viceregal Lodge – and I wanted to jump out of the car and run the rest of the way! The House is like a colossal Scottish Hydro; in fact they call it the Old Hydro. The gardens in front of the house are a mass of huge hydrangeas and round the portico the loveliest white and blue creepers. Just as we drove up Brucie ran out, it was so wonderful to see him, he looked so brown and well. Little Jeannie came trotting after him and started kicking up the most awful shindig, jumping up and down – a lovely welcome – I was so happy.

We went into the enormous panelled hall, which stretched up through two galleries to a glass ceiling. On the far side of the hall was a huge fireplace – most glorious bowls of flowers everywhere – and weapons of every description on the walls. I was so excited that I could hardly speak – it was all so wonderful. A wide staircase went up on one side to the galleries above. At one end and along a wide passage from the hall is the ballroom, from which you look out on to the fabulous gardens, and beyond, the mountains. The house seems to be perched at the very edge of the bluff it is built on.

Some of the ADC's appeared, it was so nice to see them again. One of them had just crawled down to breakfast. Brucie and I sat with him and annoyed him, at least I did by eating some of his toast, eventually in protest, coffee and toast was ordered for me. Brucie then took me up to my room. It looked out on to the mountains which by then were being slowly enveloped by mist. I was next door to Felicity. We both had yapping dogs; her's annoyed me as mine annoyed her, which we thought rather funny.

I started to unpack but it was wrested from me by an enthusiastic house bearer – I had forgotten where I was! so stopped. Brucie and I then sat and conducted operations. Later I had a bath and changed. I went down to the ADC room where there was a roaring fire. We foregathered in the hall before lunch at 1.25 and waited for their Ex's to appear One of the ADC's went to collect them. I must say they have to make a most dramatic entrance every time as they have to walk along the gallery and downstairs in full view. They were very sweet to me and very welcoming. I had to sit next to H.E but Brucie was on my other so I was quite happy, though I have to say I don't find the Viceroy in the least intimidating.

No one except the Viceroy and the Governor is allowed to use cars in Simla. It is built on such a gradient that the roads might collapse – so everyone uses rickshaws. They have a fleet of them at the House and their coolies (four to a rickshaw, two in front and two at the back) wear blue livery with red sashes and blue pugrees, and of course the Viceregal cipher embroidered in red on the front of their tunics. After lunch Bruce and I took a rickshaw into the town, and got the diamond put back into my ring – I felt lost and undressed without it – while we went shopping waiting for it to be done. The centre of Simla is The Mall, where all the shops are, there is no pavement and the road narrows and widens according to the lie of the buildings. A lot of the shops are open to the street, with some shopkeepers plying their trade on the street outside their shops – jewellers making their intricate pieces – barbers shaving or cutting their client's hair – the dentist attending to his patient – all crouch on their hunkers as they work. The red hot braziers with something cooking or the sickly smell of rich sugary cakes fills the air – rickshaws going to and fro with the trotting coolies carrying the memsahibs, or others, here and there,and general hubbub – a lovely sight. The street was full of movement and of course, as there were no cars, it became a kaleidoscope of colour and bustle.

Later we walked along the ridge on which the house is built and looked down into the valley below. There were many hilltops below us, and above was an awesome sight looking at the unfolding peaks rising skywards as far as the eye could see. First of all they are covered in trees and then as they rise higher ridge after ridge, they become bare and rugged and their summits glisten in the sun. The play of light over everything was exquisite. It is all really quite unbelievable. We were at 6000ft and the height made me feel very odd so poor Bruce had to pull me all the way. We came back home and then went off to see if we could see Ghandi. He was about to break up the meeting at his house at that time, so we decided to join in with all the Indian throng, Brucie was determined that I should see him. There were crowds of Indians outside his house. Brucie suddenly pushed me forward to peer over the garden wall and there was the old boy making an appearance. He was exactly like his pictures dressed in his dhoti, which didn't cover all that much of him, and that funny little pinched up face. We expected Indian students nearby to cry out 'Quit India' at us, but nothing so exciting happened! All the other Congressmen were leaving as we turned to go. It was most interesting and exciting.

We eventually got back about 7.30, had a very welcome drink, and changed for dinner. I again, and for the last time sat beside H.E but again I was lucky – whoever made out the table plan put Bruce next to me to hold my hand. After dinner Felicity, Her Ex and I had a girl's corner and we chatted, mainly about underclothes! – which was most enlightening! Fortunately Archie John , who had gone back to Delhi, phoned, so their Ex's left and the party was broken up temporarily. They came back, said goodnight and retired. We were left in peace.

Next morning I had breakfast in bed and got up about 9.45. As we were all going to church. I put on my uniform it having the only hat I possessed. We all went in cars; Bruce, Hugh Euston and I went in the first car being the least important! followed by other guests, then family and finally the Viceroy and Vicereine brought up the rear. It was a very nice service. H.E read the lesson and a wonderful man, a schoolmaster, preached a most spirited and dramatic sermon. Then back for lunch, this time with us in the rear of the cortege!

After lunch I changed and Bruce and I went for a long walk – it was so sunny and warm. We walked right down the twisting wooded path into the valley below the house, and got back about 5.30. I felt tired but so well and so very happy. We were going out to dine and dance in the Club, but decided we'd done enough for one day. Maudie and Douglas Currie *(Military Secretary to the Viceroy)* had asked us and Felicity along for a drink, so we all changed and walked down to their house, which was a short walk away, through the gardens – the sun was just setting and a huge rainbow stretched across the sky and all its colours were reflected on the surrounding hills. Here and there lights from the houses, scattered over the hills, were twinkling. As the sun disappeared out of sight it sent up a golden light which silhouetted the black hills, and great dark grey and black clouds were rolling up. We stayed until about 9 o'clock and walked back our way lit by the moon, and its calm light seemed to caress us. We had dinner by ourselves in front in the fire in the ADC room, it was very peaceful.

I got up immediately after breakfast on Monday, when I got downstairs I met the M.S.V. who was surprised to see me around so early – it was 10 o'clock! – I was more than shocked to hear that Her Ex lounged about in bed until mid-day, as did Felicity. What a waste of a lovely day. Brucie says he is pretty shocked as well.

We set off that day to go and have lunch with the Spens' who have a house about 6 miles away and 2000ft further up the mountainside – but it took us two hours to get there. We went in the rickshaw so far, but it was so steep that we got out to give the coolies a rest. We saw the most incredible sight on our way – a coolie with the most colossal load on his back. He had a piece of cloth round his forehead and tied to the load, and was bent double with the weight. Sweat was visibly dripping from his brow; it was a ghastly sight, though I am told that this is quite normal. The villages we passed through were pretty dirty, and tiny children, with sores, filthy and with bedraggled hair, wandered naked on the road well versed in the art of begging which they are taught at a very early age.

Someway from the Spens' the coolies said they wanted some water, so we got out and started to walk hoping that they would catch us up. We didn't think it would be too far, but the road zig-zagged towards a ridge, and Brucie told me cheerfully that Wildflower, their house, was behind that – Phew – However, as a consolation it was a beautiful walk, heavenly pines and the deep valley dropping sheerly on our right – mountains with the sun shining through the clouds and mist slowly creeping up. We were now at about 8000ft. I got very hot and Brucie pulled me up. The way seemed never ending and it got later and later. We were supposed to be there at one o'clock and at 1.30 we seemed miles away. Bruce said that we must make it a matter of pride to get there by 2 p.m! We eventually got to the gates and there facing us was a drive at an angle of it seemed 45 degs! – I could have died – however we arrived, hot and dripping and my legs shaking with fatigue, on the dot of 2 p.m. It was good to see the Spens' again; I missed them a lot when they left to come to Simla during the hot weather. We were given a drink, which we put down very quickly and tried to pull ourselves together. We then went to have lunch. One whole wall of the dining room is window, and the house being perched on top of the mountain, we could look right down to the valley below and the hills beyond. After lunch we sat and talked, I'm afraid I was dying to close my eyes and fall asleep. We left just after five and walked quite a long way down, with the coolies pulling the rickshaw behind us. I would not have relished being pulled down that steep slope with the coolies having to use themselves as brakes – terrifying. As we approached Simla it started to teem with rain and we arrived home rather wet, about seven. But we hadn't nearly finished the day. We bathed and changed and set off again to dine and dance by our selves. It was lovely going along the road into Simla and seeing all the lights twinkling from the houses on the mountainside, and the last pinky mauve colours streaking across the evening sky. We had a lovely time and got home about midnight.

Next day we took a picnic lunch with us and went in the fruit lorry which goes twice a week to the fruit plantations, belonging to Viceregal Lodge, to bring back fruit for the house. It was heaven out there, miles away from everywhere. We were right on top of the world, surrounded by peach, apple and apricot trees. We walked up a good bit before we had lunch. We made pigs of ourselves on a basket of peaches that was presented to us by one of the malis, then we lay in the sun and slept it off. We started back and sang all the way back to the lorry. Just before we set off we stood and watched an Indian peasant making his meal. The oven was made of mud, and the pot of food he was cooking appeared to be potato peelings and some sort of green leaf. He produced tin after tin of spices and ladled spoonfuls of each into the mixture. A little boy started pounding chillies with a stone and all this went into the pot. The two of them giggled madly at our interest. I bent down to smell the concoction and was blown nearly sky high with its pungency. We climbed back into the van and set off home. It was still quite early but we didn't want to be too tired before the great dance that their Ex's were giving that evening.

We got back about 4.30 and had tea with the others. No one was looking forward to the evening, they said that every time they looked at the guest list they got more depressed! I knew from all that that it would be a wonderful dance. It always is if you start by thinking how awful it will be. We went to have a look at the ballroom – it looked lovely. There was only a small part cleared for dancing. The alcove where the orchestra would be, was floodlit, and at one end the tables were laid with gleaming white cloths and glistening silver and glass, and gilt chairs. The other end was a sitting out area with armchairs and sofas. The huge portraits were lit from below and the beautiful chandeliers sparkled. There were flowers everywhere – it looked like fairyland.

We tested the floor, which was like glass, we put our small dogs on a piece of cloth and dragged them about – they loved it! We collared some nuts that were being brought to the tables. We were starting to behave rather childishly, but it was fun. We all had to appear at nine and had drinks while waiting for Their Ex's who appeared just before dinner, and the orchestra started playing.

After dinner was finished we danced – it was simply wonderful. Bruce got most of the lights put out except those for the orchestra, those lighting the Portraits and the candles on the dining tables, and it all looked very romantic. After Their Ex's retired we all started enjoying ourselves. Brucie was in great form and we were able to dance a lot together – I loved every minute. It finished about 1.30, but – oh – I did enjoy it all so much. Sadly though, it was my last evening.

Next morning Bruce and I walked down into the town to do some shopping, but there was nothing worth buying. After lunch as Their Ex's were departing, Bruce shoved me forward to say goodbye. H.E was sweet 'Well', he said, 'I don't suppose we'll see you this evening Susan – have you enjoyed it?' Her Ex said that she would see me later. We did nothing most of the afternoon, as it was misty and wet. It cleared later, and as Ghandi was coming to see the Viceroy, we decided to hang around. Photographers were all over the place. About half an hour before he was due Bruce, George Cruikshank, Freya Stark,[1] who was also staying in the house, and I all sat on the portico steps and waited. George suggested to the photographers that they should take our photos – and two of them jumped to it. It was fun. We were to scram when we were alerted that the old boy had arrived at the gates. This was the fateful day when the whole plan for Independence put forward by Wavell, fell through. Jinnah had been to see H.E. and put a spanner in the works.

After tea, just before we were getting ready to leave, I was summoned to the presence! I made Brucie come with me, but she was very sweet, and it was the first time I haven't been a little scared of her. She has a way of talking with her eyes closed, and it is very off-putting. 'This is very sad,' said Her Ex with her eyes tight shut, 'I do hope you have enjoyed yourself". I told her just how much I had. I was told then to hurry up if I wanted to catch my train! I curtseyed and as I turned to go my foot caught on a rug, I regained my balance and tripped out of the room. Brucie closed the door and we both had to stifle our hysterics!

Freya Stark came back to Delhi with me. She had been staying off and on with the Wavells for some months, I think she was doing some secret work. She is so sweet and most interesting – she is obviously a very remarkable woman. She told me that she had been very badly burned as a child and that was why she wore her hair low on her forehead on her right side to cover the scar.[2] She told me all about her young life in Italy and some of her adventures. I was fascinated. We left by car about 6p.m. I felt so depressed . . . Bruce sweetly arranged that the bearer I had had while I was

[1] Freya Stark – A well known writer and traveller. This was my first meeting with her – she had developed blood poisoning from a small wound on her ankle and had been confined to her bed during the time I was in Simla – her ankle was bandaged and had a neat little bow at the front, she said that if she had to wear a bandage it might as well look pretty!
[2] I can't think why she told me she had been badly burnt, aparently this was not so – she had caught her hair in some machinery when she was a young girl, which had torn her scalp from one side of her head. She later, in the thirties, had some cosmetic surgery on the scars on her temple and eye.

staying should come down with us to Kalka to look after my luggage, and me, and see us on the train. He did everything for us, laid out our bedding and generally nursemaided us. A driver and car met us at Delhi . . .'

Delhi Letter to Bruce July 12th
'. . . Freya and I had a very comfy journey down . . . I did so hate coming away. I was so miserable that I forgot to say goodbye to our Jeannie . . . I think Mr Maiden *(who was on the train with us)* is a wonderful old man. He came and chatted with us – also gave us a detailed recipe of how to make a bread and butter pudding, which later appeared – to be eaten! We got to Kalka eventually at 10.10. It was a long journey but Freya is a wonderful person to talk to. Everything was arranged for us on the next lap thanks to you and we were met at Delhi . . .

I had lunch with her today and some peculiar old man called Guy someone or other in the External Affairs Office, who was rather like a mad Chelsea arty person. He talked exactly like Hugh's imitation of the 'Punja'. There was also a young intelligentsia called Freda, who rather frightened me with her extraordinary knowledge of anything from Arabic politics, religion of every race from the year dot, rising outlaw students – their theories of life, doctrines and the Indian mind from sweepers upwards. To say nothing of the arts of the ages. I sat back agog and aghast and quite unable to cope – but had my mind improved considerably, as well as amused at the 'museum piece's' rhetorical efforts. The amount of things he 'regretted and deplored' was hardly true.

I staggered back to work at 3.45, feeling rather pleased I was not part of the intelligentsia and that Maiden's recipe of bread and butter pudding was more in my line. I have written to Her Ex and enclose it, I hope you think it's all right.

I still think the little act of the chaprassi running down the hill with my laundry was one of the funniest things. *(he was chasing after the car as we left)* . . . Longing for Monday . . .'

Viceregal Lodge Simla
July 14th
'Just got your letter . . . I too am miserable . . . So glad you had lunch with Freya – she really is a sweet person, isn't she – although she surrounds herself with the most amazing people . . . Will be clocking in about tea time on Monday, so look out for the plane, a great silver fish with a green line down it – breathing fire and brimstone. The Conference has finally broken

up – very amicably – and we have buried the corpse of yet another British good intention. At any rate they have all had a trip to Simla at Government expense! And they all seem highly delighted that it wasn't a success! Your letter has been duly delivered to the Burra Cheese – who is beaming. We have just had a letter from Charles Lane *(General)* saying that SAC was going to keep a horse in the Bodyguard Lines and was going to arrange it through Mackie. We scratched our heads and eventually remembered that it must be through Brigadier Mackie and not 3rd Officer S.M. Mackie! But it kept us guessing for a long time . . . all my love darling, until Monday'

Brucie arrived back on the 16th, so we could celebrate his birthday together on the 19th and he had arranged a dinner party at V.H in the Tiger Room. I took the afternoon off and we had lunch together and were very noisy – Bruce was in a crazy mood. Afterwards we went to see a film called 'Practically Yours', then made pigs of ourselves, having two iced coffees and an ice cream, I felt very sick. Afterwards I was deposited at the mess and got Christine to sympathise with me and my sore tummy.

A car was sent for Christine and me just after eight and took us up to V.H. where we had a very jolly dinner party – drank champagne – made rather a noise – but we forgave ourselves.

At the end of July there was a Governor's conference – all the Governors descended from far and near and the Viceroy's House was hotching with them. Bruce and the other ADC's were flying around and being very busy – for three days I hardly saw him. Many things have happened – an election at home and a Labour Government in power – the atomic bomb dropped in Japan, and at last the end of the war. So starts the business of sorting out the mess that this ghastly war has left. My brother Ninian will I hope have survived the horrors of being a p.o.w. of the Japanese and be returned to his family. Meanwhile we wait to hear. Poor mummy will be overcome with anxiety until he is found. As well as elation, there is a strange feeling of disbelief and a sort of emptiness.

About this time Joan and Michael Spens were posted home which was a great sadness for me. I had come to think of them as big brother and sister – and Patrick was to have been my page.

In the middle of August, I was suddenly ordered to go on leave and then report back to Kandy. This was followed by frantic signals to and from Kandy. The upshot was that a Brigadier Benoy had reported me as overreaching my position by altering his routeing of a signal! Why I wasn't rebuked by him if he thought necessary I don't know, or why Heather didn't ask me for an explanation before sending such a devastating signal. Firstly how was one supposed to go on leave, just like that, and to where? She knew that our wedding plans were in train. Everyone intervened; General Lane, and even Wavell, privately, queried the necessity of the action – and in the end Charles St Quintin, who had replaced Micky Hodges as Signal Officer-in-Chief, flew up to sort things out. What a storm in a teacup.

H.E. was summoned back to the U.K. by the new Government and he left on 24th. He took Brucie as his ADC so that he would be will be able to see his father – it is 5 years since he last saw him – it would be wonderful for them both. There was a rumour, Brucie informed me that as his tour as ADC was about to finish, they might leave him there and I would follow and we could get married in the UK. This was devastating – I was still in WRNS and would have no idea when I might be repatriated and anyway all our friends were here, and the date, 23rd October had been provisionally arranged. Brucie said that he wouldn't play, and we thought Queenie was behind it. I went to the airport to see them all off, when I said good bye to Wavell I was near to tears – curtseyed and said 'you will bring him back won't you?' Douglas Currie brought me home and in the car I voiced my fears, and he said that they may be true. 'But they can't do this' I said, 'Bruce will fight it'

He told me not to worry that he was sure things would be alright

24th August
Sir John and Lady Colville have arrived to take over as Viceroy in Wavell's absence, and have asked me to come and stay while Brucie was away which was wonderful. My room looks out onto North Court and I am very cosy and have my own bathroom!

Viceroy's House
August 24th
'... The world is very empty without you ... I felt so proud and happy as you took off – though I must have looked far from it. Proud that it is me who has your love and happy because of your confidence in what you are doing. I know too how proud and happy your father will be to have you back again – and what it will mean to you. I remember many months ago how you said how you longed to see him, and how it has preyed on your mind ever since ...'

You made a wonderful take off. I watched the plane as it stood on the runway waiting for the other plane to depart – and wondered where you were. I saw Felicity but could not see you. I longed to have wings and fly too! You nearly blew me off the runway as you taxied back past us to take off, I had to hang on to my skirts to preserve my maidenly modesty! Douglas was so kind – he came back with me and told me everything that you had told me, before you left. He told me to go on with arrangements and not to worry. I shall take his advice'...

Viceroy's House
August 25th
'... Lady Colville is so sweet though I think rather nervous. She asked if I would go for a walk with her, and when I met her to go off, I bobbed to her – she was after all acting Vicereine – and she was really quite embarrassed ... I felt so overcome this evening when Rhamet suddenly appeared – I could have thrown my arms round his neck – he asked me how the Sahib was and he made a great gesture to show that you'd flown away! Jeannie has just put her little head on my knee with such a sad look – it is for you, she is wondering where you are – I've told her you'll be back very soon – she has now trotted off and is lying flat on the ground and going to sleep!

The Colvilles are so kind and easy. He asked about you, and she said 'how sad your best boy is away'. They have asked me to stay as long as I want to. Do you think this all right? Sometimes I feel it's a little presumptive of me to be here when your are not here ...'

Viceroy's House
August 27th
'... I have been acting temporary ADC 2 today. Her Ex – who of course is also temporary acting ! – asked me to go for a stroll with her this evening. It had been pouring with rain, and the four of us, H.E. plus Colin[1] – and shadowed by the 'gunman' – ploughed through the long wet grass. She asked all about us and was so interested and is so very sweet. It felt rather strange all the same that I should be strolling round the gardens with the Viceroy of India even though just 'the acting'. I have just washed Jeannie after her muddy walk – she's quietly deposited her bone under my bed so's

[1] Colin McKenzie, ADC to the Viceroy as Brucie's replacement.

she can wake me up in the wee sma' hours chewing it. At the moment she is curled up sleeping (?) – with one roving eye open!...

Everyone is so kind. I ride most mornings with Colin or Michael.[1] Today we went out on the ridge, which in the early morning is so beautiful, and the air at that hour so cool, though you could sense the heat that was to come. We have family lunches in the small dining room. Sir John calls me Susanbrusan, which I think very amusing. I go walks most evenings with Her Ex, so I think I am earning my keep'...

Viceroy's House
September 4th
'... I woke last night to see my curtain open and a man jump onto the window seat – I was frozen with fright – but managed to find a tiny voice to say 'who's that?' Jeannie gave great voice, but before I could put the light on he'd nipped out again – being barefooted it was all very silent – I thought he would still be about and lay petrified for about ten minutes. If I wasn't such an ass as to sleep in my birthday suit, I'd have been down the passage in two two's! After much contemplation I got up and fetched my dressing gown – picked up the poker – very brave – shut and bolted my window and retired to bed again feeling rather sick. I mentioned it to Douglas Currie at lunch time today and he nearly hit the ceiling, and rushed off to raise the riot act. 'What were the chowkidars doing?' he said. (all asleep on their hunkers I imagine). It was the security of the Viceroy he was worried about.!... I was thinking that perhaps it was time I went back to the rigours of the mess – when I mentioned this to the Colvilles, they insisted that I stay until your return. Do you think I'll get spoilt living in the lap of luxury? I feel it is high time I got back to earth and became my own servant – but perhaps I'll have to do that soon enough!!...'

Three Major Generals have arrived from the Japanese prisoner of war camps. One was General Percival, who was G.O.C. Malaya at the fall of Singapore. I sat next to him at lunch and he told me the most incredible and awful stories. When they were released they brought out men who had been in solitary confinement for a year – they were filthy beyond words and their hair over their shoulders. General Percival was painfully thin. He said that he hardly knew how to hold a knife and fork, and that the luxury of sheets was indescribable....'

[1] Michael Conville ADC to Sir John Colville

September 16th they all arrived back from the U.K. It was such joy to have Brucie back and to see them all again, though sad to say goodbye to the Colvilles who had been so kind. Their ADC's too had been wonderful – particularly Michael Conville who had arranged a car for me whenever I required one and accompanied me on many occasions on my many shopping trips – They were all full of news from home – Brucie had met Mummy and Sandy and also brought the news that Ninian had been found alive. He was hospitalised in Singapore and after he was fit enough would be on his way home. Wonderful, wonderful news for us all, but particularly mummy who had been on her own through five years of anxiety and only two letters from him – one a p.c. saying that he was a p.o.w., (it arrived six months after he had been taken in Singapore). She wrote every week – which was all that she was allowed – and one of the few letters he received was written in Aug 1943. We were all together when I was on leave before joining Combined Operations HQ – all of us added a couple of lines to her letter – so he knew on that date that we were all still alive.

The 23rd October was now definitely the date of our wedding to be held in the Church of the Redemption *(now a Cathedral)*. Bruce wrote to the Bishop of Lahore asking him if he would marry us: he telegrammed back saying that the 23rd suited him splendidly. Brucie chose that date as it was the day the battle started at El Alamein! – Hugh Euston was to be our Best man, and Bachan very sweetly told Bruce that he would give us one of the Rampur shooting lodges in Mussourie for our honeymoon. The only blot on the landscape was that Brucie would be posted when he fininshed his tour as ADC in November and the thought of being parted so soon was something we tried not to think about. We had after all had more time together than most people during wartime. The Spens' were so sweet and told me that I must still think of being with them as home, and that when Brucie got his posting I should continue to stay with them. I am really so very fortunate in their wonderful friendship. From then on things started to whizz – though all I had to do was to say 'yes' to all the things being arranged on our behalf. The Wavells were wonderful and said that they would give us our reception at Viceroy's House – so all invitations were dealt by the Invitation office, flowers by the garden superintendent and all other arrangements taken care of by the Military Secretary's office. Being asked if I wanted a three or four tiered cake was the only decision I had to make!

As it would still be very hot on 23rd we decided to have the wedding at 5 o'clock, and hoped that they would not put the clocks forward before that date as that would make it rather too dark for the cine we were going to have taken – *(but change it they did. This was sad, as we did not have us coming out of the church on the film)*.

There was a Ceremonial Parade on September 23rd when General Wheeler presented the Legion of Merit to the Viceroy and the C in C, General Auchinleck. This was held on the large concourse between North Block and South Block Secretariats with Viceroy's House as the backdrop. It was Bruce's last public appearance as ADC to the Viceroy. He and Bachan, the Auk's ADC, did the honours, by accompanying General Wheeler when he inspected the troops on parade. I was very proud of him.

October 1st
A large dinner party of about seventy was held at V.H this evening, mostly for the Indian Princes, I was at the far end of the table and Brucie on the other side away down at the other end. I sat next door to Sir Arthur Lothian, the Resident at Hyderabad and on my other side was Brigadier Nepean. It was all very impressive and colourful. There were seventeen Maharajas and their accompanying Staff Officers, – in all, I see from the guest list, *(which I still have)* there were eleven girls to fifty-seven fellows!!

From then on I was in a haze of happiness, and life was quite hectic. My bridesmaids Christine Guthrie *(laterLeob)* and Suzanne Marshall *(later Wainwright)* were a tower of strength, and such fun, I was lucky to have them around me.

Finale

November 2nd letter to my mother

'I went to stay with the Spens' on 18th October. I had done no work at all for about ten days – happily my relief, Joy Elms, who was not only jolly but thoroughly efficient, had arrived – I used to go up to the House and write thank you letters, or buzz about town having fittings or shopping wildly. In the last few days presents poured in and I was writing nearly twenty letters a day.

Lady Spens said I was to have breakfast in bed every day, which was wonderful. The first morning I fell asleep after breakfast and didn't wake up till nearly eleven. Bruce had phoned with an SOS for me to go up and help. I arrived to find him moving all the presents, which were making his room into a shambles, into an empty room next door. When that was done I sat down to more letter writing. Later I collected Christine from Jaipur and on to have the last fitting of my and the bridesmaids dresses. Christine was in cracking form having just got back from a fortnight in the hills. Everything was wonderful and the two of them looked so sweet. We got back from our fitting session about 6.30 and I went back to the House to see Bruce and run off a few more letters, and got back to the Spens' with little time left to change before 8.30. – The Spens' were giving a large dinner party for us – Bruce and Charles Rankin collected Christine, Suzanne and Joy and brought them along. It was a lovely party and I enjoyed it a lot, though I hardly saw or spoke to Bruce and we were far away from each other at dinner – but I was in such a daze that I wouldn't have noticed if he'd been sitting next to me or not!

As I wanted to belong to the same Church as Brucie, I was received into the Anglican Church next morning. We decided that it was the best thing to do, and the Bishop of Lahore advised it as well. Sir P and Lady Spens said that they'd come and support me and so did Hugh Euston. Bruce sent a car for us at 7 o'clock and he and Hugh were at the church to meet us.

The service – which was very High Church – was held in the tiny Lady Chapel. The reception Service took place just before Holy Communion. I was terrified of going up and doing my stuff alone – Brucie, the darling, came with me and answered all the responses with me – it was wonderful and a very lovely little service. Afterwards I went back with Bruce for breakfast and more letter writing. In the evening we went for a walk and finished up at the church where we met the organist. We were up in the organ loft and the church was quite dark except for a shaft of light, which spread across the chancel. The organist played through all the hymns we were having – *(The bridal procession hymn was 'The King of Love may shepherd is' – my mother's special request – then 'Lead us heavenly Father lead us', 'O perfect love' finally a solo voice sang 'God be in my Head' – which I always find very moving. While we were in the vestry the organist played 'Jesu joy of man's desiring')* and gave us a recital into the bargain – it was simply wonderful. We got back about 7.30 – Bruce was on duty, so I shot back to Akbar road for dinner.

Next day Brucie went shooting – he felt that he shouldn't go as there was so much to do, but I was so glad he did as it would do him so much good to get right away. I got up rather late and started to pack, without much success and proceeded to unpack again. I brought Lady Spens up to see my trousseau and she was so sweet – I adored showing off everything and did so when in the Wrennery with the slightest encouragement and sometimes without. If Christine came into our room and found me with another victim it was -'God, she's at it again' – I went up later to the pool where Maudie and Douglas were having a lunch party. After lunch I went to try and see about our flowers, or rather what they were giving me, but no one could raise the gardener so I went home.

We were going up to have dinner with the Auk in the evening. I was changing when Bruce arrived to pick me up. I didn't realise that he'd come straight from his shoot, and found him patiently waiting with the day's dust on him and filthy muddy boots – so we had to get our skates on. We thought that we were dining quietly with the Auk, but when we arrived, a little late, found that it was a huge party and we had never seen the Chief in such wonderful form. There was buffet supper on the verandah, and afterwards dancing. We had arranged with the Bishop, who had arrived that morning, that we should go back to the House after dinner to go over the marriage service with him. The dancing started after 10 p.m. which rather upset our calculations. The Auk heard that we were going to slip away and as we were sneaking off he called to us – 'mind you come back'!

We had a cosy session with the Bishop, who is a very impressive figure, fatherly and perfectly sweet. We settled the service deciding to have the new version with the old vows. He was very apologetic that he could not get any more of the white prayer books which he used to have specially bound – these he would use at the service and present to the bride afterwards, which I think rather a lovely thought. Afterwards we dashed back to the party though by this time we were a little weary – however we enjoyed it immensely.

Next day 22nd was chaotic – but such fun as it all has been. Two Black Watch Officers and two pipers have arrived – it was really very exciting to have them. More letters to be written – we have been so lucky and had some lovely presents, there are some terrible ones as well which caused us great amusement and much scratching of heads as to what we should say thank you for! I went shopping later while Brucie went about some other business. Christine and I went to the dressmaker and collected everything and later we had a late and very scrappy lunch

Our next rendezvous with Bruce was for the rehearsal that evening at 5.15. which was most exciting – I had been beside myself with excitement for weeks anyway. Everyone arrived; the Bishop, Spens', bridesmaids, pipers, Hugh and the two Black Watch Officers. Sir Patrick made me start at the church door – The Bishop told me to take my time and that everything could wait until I was ready. I walked up the aisle of the empty church, while Bruce and Hugh stood grinning at the altar steps. Afterwards we all went back to the House, Christine came to see all the presents as she had to help the next morning to arrange the display. The garden superintendent came to measure us for our head-dresses – no one knew quite what they were doing – and no one ever seemed to be in the same place at the same time – absolute shambles. The lights were being put up in the trees in the garden and we went out to see what they were like and then I went off to the room where the presents were to inspect a sample bowl of flowers, which were absolutely gorgeous. There were four large marble basins, built into the walls at each corner, which were going to be banked with huge arrangements of flowers and lit from behind. I was thrilled with it all.

A lot of time and argument was spent over deciding just where the band would play during the reception and we were all rather exhausted so went back to the ADC room for a quick one. I whisked off Christine to see the presents so that she had some idea what was from whom and that the cards wouldn't get too mixed up. When we got back to join the others, the

ADC room was a funny sight – everyone in the House, except of course their Exs, had congregated there. Some were lying on the floor ,including Bruce, the sofas were packed with live masses and all were consuming large drinks, and there was general pandemonium. In the middle of all this Billie Henderson walked in with a huge bag, clinking ominously, ready to take to the party that the boys were having for Brucie – poor Bruce didn't want to go a bit. I heard later that the bag contained champagne, wine and kummel, eight bottles in all and all was consumed – all made merry and I got very merry! Time was getting on so we thought we'd better depart, and the boys thought they had better go and change. Brucie dashed from the room and seconds later appeared in the doorway and called for me in a commanding voice 'Here – I want to speak to you!' I went, amid roars of laughter from all the others and from us as well. We said goodnight to each other. Christine and I left with a warning that if Bruce felt awful next day we'd never forgive them – we departed with laughter ringing in our ears.

Christine came back and dined with me at Akbar Road, and afterwards she came up and helped me pack. In fact the darling did it for me. She also spent ages helping me to fix my veil – I couldn't make up my mind whether to have it over my face or not. Eventually we decided not and she fixed it accordingly and pacified me by saying it looked lovely like that. – Poor patient Christine she had to tell me the next morning that it looked lovely over my face – I had got out of my bed at midnight and unpicked all her work as I had decided to be traditional and have it over my face!

I woke the next morning with the lark and jumped out of bed to try my veil on. I was standing in front of my long mirror with my veil on my head when the door opened and in walked Lady Spens to kiss me on my wedding morning. It suddenly occurred to me what an absolute ass I looked standing there with nothing on but my veil – however the poppet didn't bat an eyelid. She kissed me and wished me much happiness, and gave me an Anthology of Verse inscribed 'To Susan on her Wedding Day 23rd October 1945 with dearest love H. Mary Spens' – I could have cried. I will not ever forget their love and support – I truly love them.

Christine arrived about 10 oclock bringing up a few things of mine from the dressmaker, then she shot off to the House to supervise the laying out of the presents. Brucie phoned me and said that everyone felt simply awful after the stag's party except himself and he felt wonderful. (He didn't tell me that Mrs White *(the housekeeper)* had found him fast asleep at 10 o'clock and pulled all the bedclothes off him!)

Christine arrived back at lunch time in fits of mirth. When she arrived she found Brucie in the ADC room playing the ass and banging a gong that had just arrived as a wedding present. He also told her that for the first time since he had been there her Ex had got up for breakfast. Brucie took her along to the room where the presents were but before they got there, she heard a loud organising voice from within. She told Bruce to go and scout to see how the land lay. She hid behind a pillar as Bruce went in. Next thing she heard her name being called and Bruce came and hauled her out. She had forgotten about the tablemats, which she had perched on her hand like a waiter's tray, and sallied forth to meet Lady Wavell. Still with the mats perched on her hand, she did her curtsey – and was then subjected to cross questioning by the old girl who spoke to her, as is her habit, with eyes tight shut. Christine was tickled pink and fairly brought the house down when her Ex had gone.

After lunch we both had a rest – tea was going to be brought at 3.30. I fell fast asleep which was extraordinary, I didn't even hear Christine moving about, or having a bath though the door of the bathroom was open. When she woke me I wouldn't believe her when she told me I'd fallen off.

Strangely enough I was quite calm and collected. Suzanne arrived at 4.15 with all the bouquets, and I hadn't even begun to be ready. My bridesmaids looked lovely and I was very proud of them both – they could not have been nicer, more fun or given more moral support than they did – I am very lucky to know them. Three pairs of hands tried to fix my veil – it was on – and came off again – and once more put in position by one pair of hands – my own. I decided at the last moment that I wouldn't wear any flowers in my hair – and at last we were ready. Christine, Suzanne and Lady S all went off and I got restless while I had to wait for the car to come back – when it did it was too early to start – it only took four and half minutes to get to the church via Viceroy's House. However I couldn't wait so I suggested we went off and made a detour to take up the time, which we did. We had to finish up at North Court to make sure that their Ex's had left. It struck 5 o'clock just as we got there – their Ex's car had gone so we whizzed on.

The Bishop was waiting on the steps to meet us when we arrived at the church. He was so sweet – he said 'We are all waiting for you Susan, take your time, there's lots of it.' When we got inside the door, Charles Rankin, who was an usher, was standing there, I caught his eye – he gave me a big wink and whispered 'it's another 40 years'.

I cannot tell you how terribly, terribly proud I was as I walked up the aisle – I thought I'd be terrified with all the mass of people – but I wasn't

– I didn't even see them. When I got to the top of the aisle Brucie was standing there looking so handsome in his dress uniform – I nearly popped all my dress buttons with pride. He came to meet me and smiled – I felt absolutely calm and just terribly happy. When we walked up to the altar after the service, I took Bruce's hand – as per instructions – but he whispered desperately 'don't hold my hand I've got to keep my bloody sword in place'. After the address and the blessing we stayed kneeling, and a solo voice sang '*God be in my head*' which was wonderful and very moving.

We had had great arguments beforehand about curtseying to their Ex's – some said not at all and others to do so in the vestry – but they also said that she would probably sail in like a ship and throw her arms round me. When we were in the vestry she appeared and made towards me with her arms outstretched with a 'My dear Susan you look simply lovely.' I seized one of her hands and sank in a curtsey thereby avoiding the head on collision and what might have been an embrace. H.E. was sweet. We were both determined not to rush down the aisle – when the music opened and the sound soared upwards, I just wanted to burst into tears of happiness. It was thrilling when we got to the doors and the pipers struck up – how I love them – Flash bulbs were flashing and we stood there just drinking it all in while the pipers played '*The Highland Wedding*', it was really an incredible moment.

We came back through South Court and straight to the rooms that had been given to us to change in. After comfort stations, champagne was waiting for us, which we drank with great ceremony and great joy. And then off to the reception. It seemed never ending – I was thrilled when I saw Charles St. Quintin – he had flown up from Kandy and brought some other of my chums for the wedding and a well timed meeting in Delhi! We tried very hard to memorise the presents and attach them to the givers – and did so quite a lot of the time. However, when Nancy Wavell *(Wavell's sister)* came along Bruce started to thank her for the lovely – ? He stopped to make appropriate signs to describe a shape with his hands – and was prompted by her 'oh it was only a small ash tray', that really did set us all off.

After we had received all the guests we went out to join them in the garden, where the band was playing old fashioned waltzes, which made a pleasing background. The cake was on a table in the centre of the lawn. After we had cut it Sir P gave a very amusing toast, after which Brucie stepped forward and said 'Your Excellencies, Sir Patrick, ladies and gentlemen – pause – thank you very much', and stepped back beside me again. It was absolutely classic and brought the house down. He had started as if he was going to make a well-prepared speech – and then that – it was heaven.

We enjoyed ourselves so much that we didn't want to leave – but we were torn away to be photographed and change. Jeannie was brought to us and had a blue ribbon tied round her neck – she looked simply adorable. One of the pipers arrived, and when we were ready he struck up and led us off – and the noise fairly resounded in those huge marble halls. Jeannie trotted beside him with her little head looking up at this strange man and the noise, we were in fits of laughter and needless to say, so was everyone else. We got into the car and were just starting off when a chap-prassi appeared bearing a small dish of rather smelly meat and a large bone and plonked it on the floor of the car – Thus the crazy photo taken just as we left and everyone was convulsed with laughter – this final Viceragal touch was too much!

Epilogue

After our stupendous send off we were driven up to Mussourie where we spent a fortnight in one of the Maharajah of Rampur's hunting lodges which Bachan his son kindly gave us. Everything was laid on, which was truly marvellous and we had our bearer Rhamet with us. It was in the most beautiful setting and surrounded by majestic mountains. Bachan had alerted some friends of our arrival and they were very kind. We were invited out on a shoot and off we set, but crossing a shallow river the shooting brake got stuck, there was much shouting and gesticulating, shoving and pushing, and much to our amusement all shouting different suggestions how to get out of the predicament. Eventually, hey presto, an elephant appeared from nowhere with a couple of chaps atop. It was immediately commandeered and put to, pulling us over to the bank at the other side. – my day was then made complete by being given a ride on the elephant. We were also taken out one evening looking for big game. An enormous searchlight was fixed to the roof of the shooting brake, and off we set, the light sweeping the way in front. Again there was much enthusiastic shouting and claims of seeing game, but I dare say that any self-respecting animal had long since legged it up the mountainside, and indeed we saw none. However they were all so friendly and welcoming, and we loved it. The second fortnight the Colvilles had invited us to Government House Bombay. We were put in Point Bungalow which is on the edge of the cliff overlooking the sea and was quite a miraculous place to be. We swam, sailed and lazed the days away and were marvellously entertained. We were lucky indeed.

Brucie finished his tour as ADC on 20th November. While we were in Mussourie a telegram arrived offering him the appointment as Military Secretary in HQ Batavia with rank of major, which he accepted.

We got back to Delhi, on the evening of 19th November, and went home chez Spens., where we got a lovely welcome. The next few days we spent at VH sorting our wedding presents as they were to be crated up there and sent off, which was such a huge help. Then there were a lot of farewell parties. A dinner party, which I remember particularly, was with Billie Henderson in his exotic apartment at VH, when Lady Wavell, during the course of conversation, and as usual with her eyes tight closed, asked me if I went to Bombay with Bruce. – classic. On the 24th the ADC's organised a party at the Imperial Hotel for the Supremo – who had arrived in Delhi on 23rd – Lady Mounbatten and Patricia, who was now working in our Signal Office, and their entourage. As soon as the Supremo was spotted autograph hunters began to appear – led, needless to say, by our gallant Allies the Americans. Some shook him warmly by the hand saying they were 'sure glad to be able to do so – that they had been in his Command for two years,' etc etc. it was very amusing. Lord Louis was in colossal form and danced the whole time – when my turn came he poked me in the arm saying 'come on and dance!' After that Brucie and I danced together the whole time, it was wonderful. On Sunday 25th November we were summoned to lunch at VH which was held out on the terrace. Afterwards HE presented Brucie with a signed and framed photo, and also a pair of, I'm afraid monstrous, cufflinks with the Wavell insignia in gold on white enamel, and rather large – they are still kept, though I have to say they were never worn! – but the photograph we were both proud to have.

I made my number with the office as I was going to continue to work until my release came through. Patricia Mountbatten had now joined us and was very sweet and unspoiled. My replacement, Joy Elms, was a joy with the hugest sense of humour, and we had a lot of laughs.

Bruce left on 27th November. I stayed on in Delhi with the Spens' who had become my surrogate parents. Later, on pre-release leave, I worked in Old Delhi in the Colonial Service recruiting office with Tony Grier, whom I introduced to the Spens family. This resulted in his engagement and later marriage to Pat Spens, Michael's younger sister, a very happy conclusion to my few weeks of work.

Maudie Currie very kindly asked me to stay with them for Christmas as the Spens' were going to Bikaner for the famous duck shoot (I was told that the duck are gathered into baskets and let loose in their hundreds for the guns to blast at – not very sporty), and I had a very happy ten days with them. On Christmas day we all went to church, then up to have drinks with the ADC's and lunch at the pool afterwards.

On New Year's Eve the Spens' had an enormous cocktail party and later I went off to the Imperial with the ADCs, where we had a most amusing evening. The menu was signed by everyone with suitable messages for me to send to Brucie. I still have it.

On February 6th 1946 Brucie came home on leave and after ten blissful days together he had to return to Java to await his repatriation. As I was still officially in the WRNS I would have to be repatriated from India, and the fact that we were married – but in different services – and wished to travel home together, did not carry much weight with the authorities. This was not a happy situation, however Brucie managed to pull a few strings to get himself back to India so's we could go home together. This ended some weeks of anxiety for both of us. Things in India had started to be difficult, there were riots and trains were being stopped and other frightening things, and the thought of the journey to Bombay without him was not too amusing.

Brucie got back to Delhi on 8th March and we hectically got ourselves organised, and after an endless round of farewells we left Delhi on 17th March for Bombay, where the Colvilles, once more, had very kindly asked us to stay at Government House Bombay until our ship sailed – date of sailing only approximate.

Diary
March 17th 1946
…Sad goodbyes to the Spens whom I had come to love so dearly – we had to leave at the crack of dawn and finding our car had been garlanded with bougainvillia, and blossom scattered over the seats, made us feel quite emotional – and so we drove off. We had an air-conditioned coach on the train which was wonderful – but almost too cold! – and had a couple of detective novels and 'battleships' to keep amused on the long journey…Brucie says I cheat – I don't.

It seems sad leaving behind the place where we met, and loved – and yet I am not sad – we have lovely memories of everything to take with us – but greatest of all we are together, so where ever we are will be wonderful.

March 18th
…We drew into Bombay on the dot. – the journey was luxurious to say the least and we were met by one of the ADC's. We found ourselves on the platform surrounded by our many pieces of luggage which were whisked away – and us too! We have been put in West Bungalow, which is lovely. Wandered down to the beach after lunch – Brucie played tennis later early bed..…

149

We finally boarded HMS *Strathedon* on the evening of 30th March after being very spoiled for a fortnight.

March 30th

... packed furiously until about 10.30 and whisked down to the town for last minute shopping and got back just in time for lunch. H.E. had just got back from Delhi and we said our goodbyes after lunch and fled to do yet more packing. We were finished and ready to go by 5 oclock and shot off. At the docks the Government House Babu's took over with wonderful efficiency and we walked aboard. We were, to our dismay, not given a cabin together. We of course should have realised that it would be thus – we were on a troop ship crowded to capacity with army navy and airforce person- nel and some families, being repatriated back to the U.K. all packed like sar- dines. I found myself with five other women plus three children, two of them screaming infants, while Brucie was in a small inside cabin with three other chaps and no porthole. At least we had a porthole and a bathroom with shower. We wandered about rather aimlessly and lost – it all seemed very strange and so crowded. Later some of the ADC's appeared to have a drink, which cheered us up.

March 31st

... Chained to our ship as she lies in the dock – once aboard you've had it – and so we passed the day. Nothing seemed to be doing – no canteen open, library or laundry until she sails tomorrow. In fact nothing to do – we long now to be off. Bombay does not look very pretty from an over- crowded ship in dock. We wrote letters for the boys to take ashore but they were unable to make the ship. We found it very strange that we would have to say goodnight at the cabin door.

April 1st

We started moving slowly at the crack this morning. It took us a whole hour to move down the canal. Little boys crowded round on the quayside, and our final sounds from India were the cries of 'baksheesh' as they threw oranges into the ship. Brucie and I watched the proceedings from 'B' deck. At 8.45 we were freed from the tugs and we were off on our own. We had left India.

We made plans. Brucie was to come and bring me a cup of tea at 6.30 and then go for an energetic session of PT. We would later walk our mile round and round the deck.

There were quite a few amusing moments – one of my cabin mates had two children, one about nine months old – the screamer. This situation she dealt with by shoving a nasty little rubber teat in its mouth, more often than not taken off the floor, – disgusting I thought. However I was asked one day if I would look after the child while its mother had lunch. Hardly had its mother gone than it started, and I could not comfort it – so, in desperation, I'm afraid I picked up the teat and shoved it in its mouth!

Another mother had a dusky little boy called Ashley. Passing us on the way to the dining room one morning, she said, indicating me 'Aah – shley, say hallo to auntie'! Well, well, we thought, and when out of sight had a good laugh.

While walking on deck one sunny day we came across a whole lot of women madly sewing yards and yards of material – when we asked one of them what they were doing she said that they were gathering it up to look like enormous dirndl skirts in case they might be caught by the customs for bringing in yards of cotton material! What for we asked ourselves – sheets? Curtains? *(one has to remember that there was still rationing)* – very enterprising.

We managed to occupy ourselves every day so time passed quite quickly. When we got to the Mediterranean it was bitterly cold and cloudy and I of course caught a cold, which I still had when we arrived back in England on 19th April. Brucie's mother met us at Fleet station, and took us to his sister Vena's house where I met his father, who was still walking with the aid of a stick. What an imposing lovely man he was, and so warm, with a wonderful smile and a huge sense of humour.

Bruce was posted to the War Office and we rented a house in Fleet where our first babe, David Victor, was born in November 1946. In 1948 Bruce was posted to the 1st Battalion in Duisberg Germany, at first as a Company Commander and later as adjutant to Bernard Fergusson who was commanding at that time. Duisburg was my first taste of Regimental life. As the wife of a Company Commander one of my duties was to visit Brucie's company wives who were quartered in German flats throughout Duisburg. It was my first 'tour' and I was driven on my rounds by Brucie's driver in a landrover – open at the sides – very draughty. I was offered endless cups of tea and as I was pregnant my first round was not the most comfortable. One wife was living in a flat with enormous rooms, and I had the stupidity to ask her if there was anything she needed – Oh yes indeed there was; could she have a curtain to divide the room, and the cooking utensils were all too big, could she have smaller ones, and a few other items. Feeling that I was in the exalted position to make all this come to pass, I returned to the Barracks and approached the then Quartermaster, Nobby Clark – a Lancastrian and a lovely man – and read him the list of requirements. He looked at me for a few seconds and then said 'Well she knows where she can *putt* them'. Needless to say I never asked silly questions like that again – I kept safely to matters of welfare.

There Yaya (Angela) was born in May 1949. The Battalion then moved to Berlin where we had eighteen wonderful months, in spite of the fact that Berlin was largely still in ruins and trucks were endlessly ferrying rubble to a huge dump we named Staff College Hill which was used as a nursery slope for skiers.! We had a fabulous house on the Havel and the regimental sailing boat was moored off our jetty. This meant that we always knew when it was not booked and could take it out ourselves, which was a huge bonus as Brucie loved sailing – and so did David, by now four years old. I remember one day when we were out, with a couple of subalterns crewing, there was not much wind so we were ambling along and one of them, holding David firmly by the wrists, lowered him overboard and dragged him along in the water. David thought this was the hugest fun and was quite unafraid. I was the one who was terrified and ordered that he should be brought aboard immediately. I then asked that they should demonstrate to me how quickly they could 'go about' if they had to rescue anyone who had fallen overboard – it took longer than I was prepared to accept!.

Then Scotland – Staff college – and back to the War Office. This posting inspired us to buy our own house in Fleet, which was in easy distance from London and Camberly. Here Johnnie was born in April 1955. It was then back to the Battalion, as Company Commander in Berlin then Edinburgh – Sandhurst as Instructor and back to Perth where Brucie commanded the 6/7th Black Watch. Our final posting was Belgium in S.H.A.P.E. It was here in 1971 that Brucie decided to retire and come and run Bengairn, which he loved. So ended our army life. It was several years before I stopped having itchy feet and wondering why it wasn't time to pack my bags again. It was a life I loved in spite of the fact that a new move filled me with apprehension, though I knew that within a few days of arriving at the new quarters we would have got everything into place and I would be happy again. The Black Watch was and still is 'family' and I cannot think of happier times than when we were with them..

Brucie died on 14th September 1995 and I would spend many hours

aged 74.
(b. 1921)

152

reliving our life together. We had kept all our letters and notes to each other, and my mother had kept my long letters to her – I also kept a journal while I was in India. The thought often occurred to me that I should put it all together. A computer course was the next step, followed needless to say by a computer, and off I went. It has given me huge pleasure over the four years I have been putting it together, with so many wonderful memories to relive. I hope that my grandchildren and perhaps my great grand children will one day enjoy it, no doubt wondering what a strange world we lived in – when they may have gone to the moon. Ah well, I think our world was better.

Sue died on 26 Dec 13 aged 92.

Natty Notes for Night Watches

Delhi December 1943

SPECIAL EDITION – (plaindress today, other days dress optional)

The main thing to do is to go to sleep as soon as possible and the long night can be spent in thinking up ways of making this possible. You arrive on the transport (God and WRNS officers willing) at 7, full of joy having eaten an enormous meal in five minutes. Susan always with food and thermos, I always ignore this sordid side of life and I find that the Wrens always bring mine up for me, they always have, so why stop now? You work madly till 2230 writing to your friends and tearing up the snags that have accumulated during the day. If you have a good watch on they will suddenly produce toast and jam and coffee for you and fruit; if they show no signs of feeling hungry you just go and help yourself. The RNCCO *(Naval cypher office)* usually cough up a goodly wodge of signals about 2200 and again around midnight and 0200, then peace reigns from then till about 0600 (with luck). GHQ has no feelings and send D.R.'s over at any time specially when you have just gone to sleep. Two of the Wrens usually go to sleep at a time but it depends on the work and how they feel. They take the stuff that comes off the T/P to the War Room all night so it is quite easy. I have my bed in the middle of the floor, put all the lights out but the standard, which I lift down on to the floor behind my desk so that it shows a minimum of light. You will find that if it is on the desk it shines delightfully into your eyes. Put the key of the bag in the middle of your desk and go to sleep. When the chaprassi comes with his bag of signals, you point wildly at the keys and he unlocks it and gives it to you etc. I always read them in case they are emergency ops and put these on the desk (thoughtfully in reach without getting out of bed) and go to sleep again. The tin box man does not come very often at night. You can get rather a wodge in at about 0700 when everyone really wakes up, so I don't let too much pile up. About 0745 the sweeper appears and wants to sweep, you divert him to the Wrens room and then to CSO's, by that time your relief may have come and you are spared an imitation of the Sahara on the move. When Susan does appear do not take too long turning over, this does not pay in the long run as you will have to walk home (you may know this already of course) Open the windows before you leave, it's a nice gesture. I have a typewriter in here but I do not often ormig[1] on it as usually the M/S typist copes OK, and if they are very weary and the others have nothing to do let some of the old firm help too.

If you are unhappy do ring up Miss Hayes, a delightful soul who never minds being rung up and chatted to about this and that. Don't worry if it sounds as though they were pulling the building down or having a football match on the top floor. They probably are anyway, they have been doing it for weeks, and the building stands up to it quite well.

MERRY CHRISTMAS

Wassail Prost schol, how many bottles have you got?????

This, and the next three 'Natty Notes' was written by Yvonne Stafford Curtis (known as Yvne, pronounced Yuvney, Specials,) which she wrote when on night duty to amuse and inform whoever took over from her – usually me! They were written as words flowed from mind onto the paper, and mostly without punctuation – and we all laughed as we read these outpourings of her fertile mind.

[1] Ormig – this was typing on special paper that indented the lettering which was then used for making copies

Yvne Special

SACSEA Signal Office New Delhi

Yvne Special – Alternative spelling Uffne (Urdu spelling). A good night was had by all, all telephones, typewriters and signals are covered in jam, in fact I had to stop work because this typewriter was simply jammed up there's no other word for it

I have now got three Indians[1] in here quite what they are doing is not known but one, ah one has started sweeping,the others are obviously his friends and relations (like rabbit) – two sweeping now – one has rushed to the key box and whipped one of the signal bags from out of his blanket in which he is obviously a walking advertisement for carry all with you in case moth and crickets[2] corrupt it.

They have flung open the window and a Siberian wind is blowing in from the Himalayas – I doubt if I live till breakfast. Now the party is over, and salaaming sadly they fade into the outer darkness, only to return with the dawn tomorrow. Where they go during the day I know not, probably to some cave in the hills to commune with the birds (privately have doubts about all of his being true, can this be so?) Perhaps you of great wisdom will know the answer you old finx – I phinx so too – (jolly clever that) ha ha ha I am laughing myself sick. I must go quickly so as to be in time for the transport, to be sick in till breakfast time.

And so we leave Mother India brooding under the glowing dawn, having just flung her starlit mantle away (the rude hussy). And slowly wind our way down the sacred Ganges towards the beautiful city of Agra, sitting in a little boat singing rude songs

Bye ...

Bye ...

Bye ...

Gone now

[1]Indian chaprassis (messengers) were used to carry bags with signals and documents to and from South block where the HQ Signal Office and cypher offices were. They would turn up any old time day and night. They were always swathed in blankets at night. Keys for the bags were kept at the offices in HQ and by us. The other chaps sweeping were sweepers, and did just that.
[2]Crickets – small insects that would eat your clothing or anything else handy.

A Yvne Special
Supreme Commander's Signal Office New Delhi

OIC WRNS SACSEA From Assist Deputy OIC WRNS SACSEA
Ma'am, I have the honour to submit the following report. DSO 2 arrived
on watch again drunk singing and shouting all down the passage, she's
always drunk. Next thing was that she was encouraging the wrens to sing
in fact the strains of My Bonnie Lies Over the Ocean sung out of tune
could be heard bellowing forth from the quiet calm that usually pervades
147g.[1] A very quiet night was had otherwise, except for the flash when a
body who said he was the deputy Naval Commander, rang up and said he
had an Ultra for the AOC in C. SEA[2], this rather foxed the poor old DSO,
he only wanted to know how to get hold of the Duty Stooge in AHQ to
get the AOC. Eventually he appeared up here and turned out to be the
Signal Officer EF[3] *(I think)* a wavy Lt[4] I put him on to Duty Officer TDS
(having rung up meanwhile and discovered that he was the man in AHQ5
to get hold of the AOC). So off he trotted to TDS to take the thing himself,
quite why he rang me up and came up I do not quite know except that he
may not have known how or who to contact in AHQ. He was quite affa-
ble and pleasant. No other visitors or thrills. Had two WACS typists on
duty, called Mabel and Lucille this upset me considerably as I once read a
book where there were two hens called Lucille and Mabel, apparently they
are the ones with entirely unpronounceable names, so I learned from
Bromley-Marten, so that we shall probably always have to have Lucille and
Mabel. Regret to say that we polished off the cake, can't think how that
happened – we were suddenly taken hungry and cut it in half. I wonder
how long HH[6] and Sally[7] stayed at the party? Were they carried out or not?
I expect that they just managed to keep on their feet. HH always goes flat
rather easily, must remember to warn the ranks. Pause ... One of my boy
friends[8] who is wearing so many blankets that he can hard ly move is here

[1] 147g – Our office
[2] AOC in SACSEA: Air Officer Commander in Chief South East Asia Command
[3] EF: Eastern Fleet
[4] Wavy Navy: Royal Naval Reserve, referred to thus because of the wavy gold stripes on their sleeves instead of straight as for the Royal Navy
[5] AHQ: Air Headquarters
[6] HH: Heather Hayes 1st Officer WRNS, our boss, later married to Micky Hodges
[7] Sally: Sally Dean Lt WAC *(US)* one of our Duty signal Officers
[8] Boy Friends: These refer to the chaprassis who carried signals to and from the cypher office in South Block.

plus his little box of joy, he is not one of the brains trust and looks utterly blank and does not even drift toward the key box not like those in the know, who at least know the right place in the room to stand and some (there are very few even have a slight idea what shape and sort of key is) Another one of them – this must stop – it's the EF bag trouble again, this is a tough one, he hadn't even got one blanket on. Do you think the wrens could be issued with gay wools for night duty knitting – for kitting up lost chapprassis???? Jolly good war work instead of sitting and nattering together to keep up the naval tradition I have been years trying to discover how to keep up the good old tradition but it is still wrapped in mystery to me, why should it be kept up, how high? Does it feel the cold? Why should it not be kept on a level keel (jolly little salt tang that) or on a flat bottom, to speak plain English. Why not sunk, after all sinking the old tradition sounds very good – Don't mind if I do – mine's a pint of old and mild. I have a feeling that it was manufactured by some old man in Whitehall who having knitted himself into a ball with his own red tape could see no way of explaining his misdeeds to others and keeping his dignity, other than by saying 'It's tradition Old Man' – 'done in the Navy my boy'. This will of course fox the pure blooded Englishman who is not in the Know. His mind immediately flashed back to Nelson, Collingwood, Drake and good Queen Bess. Funny how she got in here nothing to do with this at all, it must be the old tradition of cherchez la femme. This must stop and it is 0800 and I hope that I shall see a radiant Susan any moment now. Bye . . .

Yvne Special

Signal Office SACSEA Peradeniya Gardens Ceylon
July 4th 1944 2305hrs

The DSO was having a cup of something and tying to chat intelligently to the Duty Officer (Dormer) while dealing with a pile of odd looking signals. The night had so far been enlivened by crackers going off rather vaguely in the darkness and intervals but the DSO had got used to this and sat unmoved. Suddenly a WAC panted in and gasped 'The Supremo's office, it's on fire'. The DSO took another bite out of her vast sandwich and said in a nonchalant sort of way (actually her brain was working at lightening speed – buz buz buz) before she had finished eating the bit of sandwich she had in her mouth she lifted the receiver and said 'Fire Station', this would have been a great success if her mouth had not been so full, she tried again a few seconds later with better success, the switchboard said sweetly that it had already informed the Fire Engine personally some minutes before, as it had had a pigeon message some seconds before, so the DSO gave up trying to do the right thing and rushed outside to HAVE A LOOK which was what she had been dying to do, sure enough there was a red flickering glow in the Supremo's Block, it was promising to turn out a good fire. The DSO stifled her immediate impulse to go straight to the fire and enjoy it, she turned drearily to the phone again she had to tell somebody in case it took a long time to put the fire out. She rang the Supremo's Secretary[1] as she could not remember if Flags was in residence or not. Sec. SAC who apparently was just going to bed already nearly asleep, was not enthusiastic. Having told him the bare facts and promising a bigger and better bulletin later, the DSO banged down the receiver and charged out into the moonlight and pounded over to the SAC Block. Half way across the Circus she heard the fire engine clanging away behind her down the road – there was a trailer pump going well behind the real engine – they swept past and charged on down Fifth Avenue going flat out, in spite of the little DSO's plaintive cry that the fire was right under their noses.

The fire was going quietly in flag's Office, all that was happening was that the filing cabinet (wooden, Officers for the use of) was blazing merrily away. Two immensely tough U.S Military Officers and various other U.S personnel were dealing with the situation having smashed three windows

---

[1] The Supremo's Sec, Ronnie Brockman Capt R.N, now Admiral Sir Ronnie Brockman.

and a door with great abandon they heaved the offending cabinet into the garden so that the fire was rather more isolated and could play by itself. More and more US bodies kept appearing – never knew so many lived near enough at night to come to our local amusements.

The Duty Officer, who had sat during the first few minutes after the great news had broken, with his jaw dropping, suddenly realised that being a Duty Officer was not so dull, had sped out of the Signal Office and was now questioning the crowd, as happy as a bee. Irving Asher[1] suddenly appeared, as far as could be ascertained, he had come ON the fire engine *(seems curious)*. He stood in the dark of Flag's Office a sinister figure. In the flickering light from the blazing cabinet outside he dialled WHI 1212[2] sorry I mean Snake Villa[3] and told Flags[4] the sad news. It is not known what Flags said. The DSO having seen the cabinet flung into the garden and realising that all the fun was over, went quietly to finish her cup of tea that she had had to abandon, efficiently noting that the hour was now 2315 rang K.P and said "Flags, fire negative". So ends the 4th of July in the Signal Office.

I was greeted with this wonderful story when I got back from leave in India on 13th July. Irene Richardson, who was general factotum to SC, caused this fire. She was also the Supremo's arranger of dinner parties. Signed herself with a drawing of a horse's head. A lovely person. She gave me all the photos I possess of K.P and a smashing one of the Supremo.

Yvne July 1944

0

---

[1] Irving Asher was the American film Unit and a film director in Holywood
[2] WHI 1212 was the telephone number in those days of Scotland Yard in London
[3] Snake Villa, in the grounds of K.P, was Margaret and Arthur Leveson's small house
[4] Flags, of course was Arthur Leveson

Supreme Commander's Signal Office
South East Asia

1

Our Micky is a wondrous lad
Some think him good, some think him bad
But you should see him let loose hell
He does it well – yes very well

2

His deputy is none but Hal,
He is determined that he shall
Before this current week is through
Sell Army Group a plane or two

3

The leader of the girls is Heather,
Who holds the tangled threads together–
Of cyphers, signals phone and printers
And shatters Admirals into splinters

4

We had a one called Gordon Blair,
Our senior representative of air;
As such you'd think he'd like to fly;
But no! he'd walk like you or I

5

The next is one and only Sally
With all and sundry she is pally.
My goodness, you should hear her smile
It's strength is FI-YIV at a mile

6

There's Florence too, a comely wench
Who, firmly seated on her bench
Deals well with things concerning morse
While wishing she was on a horse

7

Our Major Craig has gone away,
To get promotion so they say
We wish him luck and hope that he
Will soon be back to drink our tea.

8

Our Margaret, who was once a Maude
Has struck an Inter-Service chord
As Leveson she gets all the gravy
Because she's married to the Navy.

9

We can't forget there's Jasper Vaughan
He's just plain wolf – in fact no faun
With ears concealed when on a flip
He succeeds in getting on the strip

10

A cryptic guy is old Jock Ross
Who never gives the girls a toss;
But has them in a panic when
He emerges from his den.

11

One of two Susans (she was Pearce)
Pretends from time to time she's rather fierce.
She's really rather, rather sweet.
Of course – she came from Eastern Fleet

12

The other, Mackie is the name
Thinks changing of the staff's a shame.
But Fortunes come and Fortunes go,
So she has left – but not for dough

13

There's Barbara Donovan and Joy Elms,
Who signalwards have turned their helms,
They'll soon know what it is to live
With boys and girls of Signal Div.

14

Yvonne's a lass we all adore
Who doesn't think her work's a chore,
And by her cheery wining ways,
Does much to brighten up our days.

15

Our new boss is Charles St Quentin
And he must know it takes some stinting
To keep this crazy gang in line
It took up most of Micky's time.

16

So if your signals don't get thru'
You know exactly what to do;
Or if your telephone goes dicky
You call them twerps from Craig to Micky.

Anon
S A C S E A
Kandy, Celyon 1944

1 Micky Hodges: Captain RN Signal Officer in Chief, South East Asia command

2 Hal Grant: Col U.S. Air force Deputy SOIC and driver of *Mercury*

3 Hearther Hayes: 1st Officer WRNS, HQ Signal Officer (my no2 boss)

4 Gordon Blair: Group Captain RAF Deputy SOIC at Combined Ops London and with us to hand over to Hal

5 Sally Dean: Lt WAC USA one of our Duty Signal Officers

6 Florence: another Lt WAC USA whose surname I forget

7 Major Craig: I can't remember who he was but I have to keep him in for the rhyming of the last verse!!

8 Marggaret Maude: Flt Officer RAF another DSO

9 Jasper Vaughan: Major US Airforce Co-pilot of the Mercury

10 Jack Ross, Major:. Ran the Signals and Coding Dept. He was very pompous and didn't like any of us very much.

11 Susan Pearce: 3rd Officer WRNS another DSO she joined us in Ceylon, from Eastern Fleet Colombo

12 Susan Mackie: 3rd Officer WRNS another DSO (me!)

12 Late arrivals from Eastern fleet after I had left to be in charge of the Rear Signal Office in Delhi in Oct 44. Joy Elms replaced me in Delhi when I got married in Oct 45.

14 Yvonne Stafford Curtis: 2nd Officer WRNS and a DSO

15 Charles St Quentin: Captain RN replaced Micky Hodges as S.O. I C

163

Sticking it out in the Cecil

Fighting the Nazis from Delhi,
Fighting the Japs from Kashmir,
Exiled from England, we feel you should know
The way that we're taking it here.

Sticking it out at the Cecil
For the sake of the land we adore,
But never you worry, though continents shake,
Whatever befalls, our morale will not break
Provided that Wenger's don't run out of steak –
Doing our bit for the war.

Tightening our belts at Niroula's
Taking it all on the chin
For the sake of the Nation
We suffer privation,
Just look at the shortage of gin.

We frequently feel that in England
They don't know the straits that we're in
The way that we've cried at the news reels we've seen
(They bring it so near, if you know what we mean)
And only eight bearers instead of sixteen.
Taking it all on the chin

Roughing it at the Imperial,
Proving we're sound to the core
We take the B.O.R's for rides in our cars,
Which is secretly rather a bore.

Our women, God bless 'em, their pluck never fails,
Serving out Horlicks to combatant males,
Though the rust on the teaspoons has ruined their nails,
They're doing their bit for the war.

Fighting for freedom in Simla,
Democracy's cause we defend,
With people to tea from W.S.C.
What curious people they send.

Fighting for freedom in Simla
Doing our share and much more –
We'd like to be back in our country so dear,
One day we'll return there, of that never fear.
When Germans are not so exceedingly near,
We'll be doing our bit for the war.

Doing our bit in Old Delhi,
Gad, but its grim in the Grand.
The beer that they sell makes some men unwell,
But we're proud to see what they can stand,
Fighting for freedom in India,
The freedom from want and from fear,
Fighting like hell for all we love well
That's why we rushed to get here.

Anon

The Cecil	A large hotel in Old Delhi
Kashmir,	In the Himalayas
Maidens	A popular restaurant in Old Delhi
Wenger's	A restaurant in Delhi
Niroula	A restaurant in Delhi
The Imperial	At that time *the* hotel in Delhi
Simla	The hot weather station in the hills.
W.S.C	Winston Churchill
B.O.R's	British Other Ranks

A Tribute to the Signal Office

The lords of the air in their pomp and their pride
Are scattered from Delhi to Eastern Bengal,
But they must keep in touch
With the Chinks and the Dutch
So they signal like mad
Using type X or pad
Repeating to Uncle Tom Cobley and all.

There is Slim, who is counting his bullets and beef,
While Baldwin stands by and assuages his fears
They drink Sarsparilla
At healthy Comilla
And take transport aircraft for speedy relief, then they signal like hell
At each strike of the bell
Repeating to Washington, London, Algiers,
And you must not forget
Our M.A. in Tibet
And send copies to Stilwell, Mountbatten and Pierse.

There's the Tactical Air Force all bristling for blood,
Never failing to drop all their bombs in a pattern
When they cannot remember
The fifth of November
And fear if they don't that their names will be mud,
They jump in a taxi
And signal to ACSEA[1]
Repeating to Gifford and Slim and Mountbatten.

[1] Air command South East Asia

There's Joe Stilwell who likes his Japs fried without butter
Who is usually terse and sometimes insultin'
He don't answer letters
From equals or betters
From ACSEA or SACSEA, Ceylon or Calcutta,
But we signal to ask
What will be his next task
Repeating to Stratemeyer, Gifford and Sultan

Then there's Carton de Wiart in distant Chungking
Needs a signal a minute to keep him in trim
He sends genuine dope
To the King and the Pope
And requires to be kept up to date in each thing;
So we send him a signal
Neat, brief and original
Repeating to Axiom, Baldwin and Slim.

But Margaret and Sally and Susan keep calm
They eat chocolate and sourballs and never go wrong;
While if it was me
I'm afraid you would see
The lords air grow pale with alarm
At finding their signals address to the stars
With copies in plain
To the late King of Spain
Gracie Fields, Noel Coward and Anna May Wong.

Philip Mason
Director Plans South East Asia

Abbreviations

AOC	Air Officer Commanding
ACSEA	Air Commander South East Asia
A.D.C.	Aide de Camp to the Viceroy ADC 1 was in attendance to H.E
	ADC 2 in attendance to Her Ex
	ADC 3 in attendance to guests or off duty
A.L	Arthur Leveson Lt Commander RNVR Flag Lieutenant to Mountbatten
ACOS	Assistant Chief of Staff
A.V.M.	Air Vice Marshal
B.W	The Black Watch
C in C	Commander in Chief
COS	Chief of Staff
CSO	Chief Signal Office
D.O	Duty Officer
D.R.	Despatch rider
DCOS	Deputy Chief of Staff
DSO	Duty Signal Officer
E.C	Donald Erskine-Crum Air ADC to Mountbatten replaced Hank Hanbury
ETA	Estimated time of arrival
ETD	Estimated time of departure
F.D.R	Franklin D. Roosevelt – President of the USA
H	Hank Hanbury Air ADC To Mountbatten
G.H.	Government House
H.E.	His Excellency The Viceroy
Her Ex	The Vicereine Lady Wavell
His Ex	The Viceroy
HH	Heather Hayes 1st Officer WRNS H.Q. Signal Officer
HQ DSO	Headquarters Duty Signal Officer
L.M.B	Louis Mountbatten

MH	Michael Hodges Captain RN SOIC
ML	Margaret Leveson Flight Officer WAAF DSO
M.S.V	Military Secretary to the Viceroy
N.O.	Naval Officer
P.M.	Prime Minister
R.N	Royal Navy
RNVR	Royal Naval Reserve
S.C.	Supreme Commander – Mountbatten
SAC	Supreme Allied Commander – Mountbatten
S.E.A.	South East Asia
S.E.A.C.	South East Asia Command
S.O.I.C	Signal Officer in Chief
T.O.O.	Time of Origin
U.P	United Provinces
V.H.	Viceroy's House
V.R.	Viceregal
WRNS	Women's Royal Naval Service
W/T	Wireless telegraphy
YSC	Yvonne Stafford Curtis DSO

Who's Who and What's What

Asher, Irving
   USA Film Unit SEAC and Hollywood Director

Astley Simon,Capt the Hon. 7th Hussars
   ADC to the Viceroy

Astley, Joannie the Hon.
   Viceroy's Daughter married to Simon

Auchinleck, Field Marshal Sir Claude
   Commander in Chief India

Beaton, Cecil
   Royal Photographer

Blair, Gordon Group Captain RAF
   Deputy Signal Officer in Chief Combined Ops HQ London

Brockman, Ronnie Captain R.N.
   Secretary to Mountbatten

Burra
   Great, big, important

Chaprassi
   Messenger

Chota
   Small

Chowkidar
   Caretaker, nightwatchman

Colville, Sir John
   Governor of Bombay

Coates, Peter
  Controller Viceroy's House

Cruikshank George, Capt 3rd Hussars
  ADC to the Viceroy

Currie, Douglas
  Military Secretary to the Viceroy

Currie Maudie
  Douglas' wife

Dean, Sally Lieutenant WAC US Army
  Duty Signal Officer, Supreme Commander's Signal Office

Dengue
  Tropical disease caused by a virus spread by mosquitoes

Dhersie
  Tailor

Dobie
  Washerman

Euston, Hugh, The Earl of, Capt. Grenadier Guards
  ADC to the Viceroy,
  (now the Duke of Grafton)

Erskine-Crumb, Donald, Sqdn Leader RAF
  Air ADC to Mountbatten

Faridkot House
  Mountbatten's residence in Delhi

Feng Yee, Major General
  Head of the Chinese Military Mission

Fleming, Peter
  Deception Division (brother of Ian Fleming)

Force 136
  Dealt with agents behind enemy lines

Generalissimo Chiang Kai – Shek
  General of the Chinese Army

Greenwood, Alex
ADC to Field Marshal Auchinleck, C. in C. India

Grant, Hal, Colonel US Army
*Deputy Signal Officer in Chief South East Asia
and pilot of the Mercury*

Guthrie, Christine, 2nd Officer WRNS
*Aerial Photographic Interpreter
Room-mate, friend and bridesmaid.*

Hanbury, Hank Sqdn Leader RAF
ADC to Mountbatten

Hapgift
*LMB's long haul plane – present from
General Henry (Hap) Arnold,
Chief of the American Air force, Washington*

Hayes Heather 1st officer WRNS
HQSO, 2 i/c to Micky Hodges

Henderson, Billie
Viceroy's ADC

Hodges, Michael, Captain RN
Signal Officer in Chief SACSEA

Jacob's Follies
Officer's club in Kandy, designed by Michael Jacobs

Jacobs, Michael
*Supervised arrangements in Kandy
before arrival of HQ from Delhi*

Jerram, Rear Admiral Sir Rowland
Controller of HQ

Keswick John
*Political Advisor for Chinese affairs
(also Tai Pan Jardine Matheson Hong Kong)*

Khitmatgar
Butler/waiter

King's Pavilion
Mountbatten's residence in Kandy

Kukri
Large curved knife broadening towards point

Kus kus
*Tatting made of grass, hung outside windows
and kept wet, to cool rooms*

Lane, Charles, Major General
Supremo's Deputy Rear HQ SACSEA Delhi

Leveson Arthur Lt Commnder RNVR
Flag Lieut to LMB. Married Margaret Maude

Mali
Gardener

McKenzie, Colin Capt.
ADC to Wavell arrived summer 1945

Mason Philip
Director of Plans and author

Marshall,Suzanne Capt WAC(I)
Friend and bridesmaid

Maude, Margaret Flt Officer RAF
Duty signal Officer Supreme Commander's Signal Office

Mercury
*LMB's signal plane this plane
was full of signal equipment to enable
Mountbatten to communicate with HQ while on tour*

Merrill, George
President Roosevelt's Representative in India

Merrill, Ruth
George Merrill's sister

Mountbatten, Admiral Lord Louis
Supreme Allied Commander South East Asia

Murphy, Peter
Odd job man to Mountbatten

Nimbu pani
fresh lemon squash

Overlord
Invasion of Europe 1944

Pani wallah
Water carrier

Papps, Johnnie
Controller King's Pavilion

Pearce, Susan 3rd Officer WRNS
Duty Signal Officer Supreme Commander's Signal Office

Pierse, Air Vice Marshall Sir Richard
Allied Air C in C

Peradeniya Gardens
Botanical Gardens, Kandy (HQ SACSEEA)

Pownall, Lieut General Sir Henry
Chief of Staff South East Asia Command

Punka
A long fan made of material,
like a short curtain, hung from the ceiling.

Punka Wallah
The wretched chap who would have to activate this by pulling
on a rope, usually by his toe, while sitting on he ground

Rampur, Bachan
ADC to General Auchinleck son of the Maharjah of Rampur

Richardson, Irene 2nd Officer WRNS
Personal Sec and general factotum to Mountbatten
affectionately known as 'The Horse'

Sales
Mountbatten's Marine Sgt driver

Shikar
Game keeper/shoot

Sister Anne
LMB's short haul plane

Social Rounds
Top Secret and Eyes Alone signals delivered by hand of officer

Somerville, Admiral Sir James
Commander in Chief Eastern Fleet (Uncle James)

Spens, Sir Patrick & Lady
Chief Justice of India

Stafford-Curtis, 'Yvne' 2nd officer WRNS
Duty Signal Officer Supreme Commander's Signal Office

Sillwell, J.W-General US Army
Deputy Supreme Commander & Northern
Combat Air Commander and 2i/c ACSEA (Vinegar Joe)

St Quinton, Charles, Captain RN
Replaced Michael Hodges as SOIC October 44

Stratemeyer, George Lt General USAF
Air Commander and 2 i/c ASCEA

Tonga
Two wheeled horse drawn carriage/buggy

The York
Mountbatten's long haul plane

Torch
Invasion of North Africa 1942

Trubody, 'Tru' 2nd Officer WRNS
Secretary to General 'Spec' Wheeler US Army –
always known as Tru

Uncle James
Our affectionate name for Admiral Sir James Somerville

Vaughan, Jasper Lt USAF
  2nd pilot of the Mercury

Wavell, Archie John the Hon. Black Watch
  Viceroy's son

Wavell, Field Marshall, Viscount
  The Viceroy

Wavell, Lady *(Queenie)* Viscountess
  The Vicereine

Wavell, Felicity *(Fizzie)* the Hon.
  Viceroy's daughter, worked with Peter Fleming

Wedemeyer, Al Lt. General US Army
  Deputy Chief of Staff later replaced General Stilwell

Weld, Joe.Lt Col, Marines
  Intelligence

Wheeler, *(Speck)* Lt General US Army
  Principal Administrator, later Deputy Supreme Commander

Williamson, Harold
  Surgeon to the Viceroy

Wilson Douglas Flt Lieut RAF
  Air ADC to Mountbatten

Wingate, Major General Orde
  Leader of the Chindits